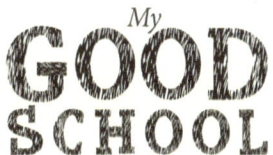

Sandeep Dutt is a school coach, bookseller, runner, mountaineer and social entrepreneur. His work for the International Award for Young People (IAYP) has been widely acknowledged all over the world. As a social entrepreneur, Sandeep works to empower young people and has been a mentor for many. His mission is to 'help schools deliver better' with a focus on building professional learning communities at schools.

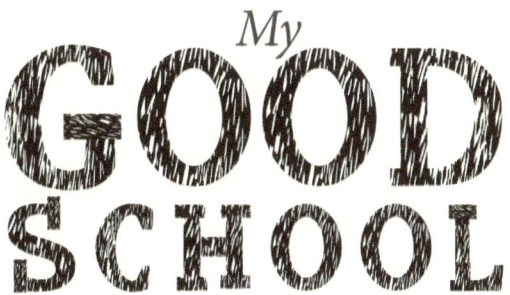

My GOOD SCHOOL

Where Passion Meets Education

SANDEEP DUTT

Published by
Rupa Publications India Pvt. Ltd 2021
7/16, Ansari Road, Daryaganj
New Delhi 110002

Sales centres:
Allahabad Bengaluru Chennai
Hyderabad Jaipur Kathmandu
Kolkata Mumbai

Copyright © Sandeep Dutt 2021

The views and opinions expressed in this book are the
author's own and the facts are as reported by him which
have been verified to the extent possible, and the publishers
are not in any way liable for the same.

All rights reserved.
No part of this publication may be reproduced, transmitted,
or stored in a retrieval system, in any form or by any means,
electronic, mechanical, photocopying, recording or otherwise,
without the prior permission of the publisher.

ISBN: 978-93-90547-40-1

First impression 2021

10 9 8 7 6 5 4 3 2 1

The moral right of the author has been asserted.

This book is sold subject to the condition that it shall not,
by way of trade or otherwise, be lent, resold, hired out, or otherwise
circulated, without the publisher's prior consent, in any form of binding or
cover other than that in which it is published.

Contents

Preface	*vii*
Foreword	*xiii*
Introduction	*xv*

Section I
The What, the Why and the How of Teaching

Why Go to School?	3
Quality in Education	6
How Your Child Learns the Best	12
Performance Scores Must Be Honest	18
People, Process and Outcomes	25
Choice of Curriculum	30
Building Schools with Quality	41
Fun in Learning, Learning Is Fun	44
Life Is Parenting	47
An Eager Child or Enthusiastic Teacher?	51
Why Teachers Are Averse to Change	56

Section II
Redefining Education and Learning

Reading at the Heart of Education	61
Innovation and Design	66
The Art of Writing in School	70

The Annual Day at School	75
Schools Must Provide Knowledge, Not Mere Information	80
Value of Liberal Arts Education	86
Humanity Must Learn Humanities	91
New Teaching and Learning Approaches	94
Freedom to Perform	98

Section III
Lessons for Life

What Education Does	103
School Bell: The First Lesson in Management	108
Going to School	112
Learning: From Isolation to Collaboration	114
Teachers Travel with You All Your Life	117
Personal and Social Development at School	123
Real-World Learning	129
Today Is the Day when You Define for Yourself	133

Section IV
School Leadership

Leadership Begins and Ends at the Top	137
Principal as the Chief Learning Leader	144
Student Leader: Mentor or Monitor?	150
Smart Teachers Make Smart Classes	155
Conclusion	160
Index	167

Preface

In 1979, I took the first-ever flight of my life to attend the International Gold Award Holders Summit, the prestigious youth awards program founded in 1956 by Prince Phillip, Duke of Edinburgh. A proud young Gold Award winner, I was flying from New Delhi to Darwin, Australia. Little did I know then, that four decades later, the editor of *The Rose Bowl*, the Doon School Alumni magazine, would call me and find my story worthy of sharing!

What is now called the International Award for Young People (IAYP) was called The Duke of Edinburgh's Award when I was at school. The Gold Award of the programme really made me find myself, and the journey of three decades of volunteering and morphing into becoming the first boy from The Doon School to become its National Director, is a story that will surely interest the teaching fraternity. Many may not know that the Award was introduced at The Doon School in the 1960s. It took nearly 50 years of existence to have a Dosco (an alumni of the school) head the Award, set up the India office and give IAYP the shape and colour we see today.

The Award philosophy has played a great role in my life, and thus the idea of taking the same to rural and faraway schools took form. How do the 4S's—Service, Skill, Sport and Study—shape our lives? Take a closer look at your school years and see how we have evolved from service to skill. If you delve even further, you will find that the 4S's are placed in the dictionary of the school in the very same order. Moving from your small family space into school starts with learning to give and share your space, your food, your things and this really is the first form of service. Yes, you acquire skills, play a sport for good health and get the full experience at school, to achieve what we call the goal of 'study'.

As Arthur Foot had beautifully put it in 1935, 'The boys should leave Doon as members of an aristocracy, but it must be an aristocracy of service inspired by ideas of unselfishness, not one of privilege, wealth or position.'

With three decades of volunteering with schools, in 2012 the search for the My Good School model took me to Bali, a village in Rajasthan. This is where we worked to build perhaps the first 'My Good School'. The Fabindia School is indeed a shining example of aristocracy of service. This school's mission is to provide access to high-quality education for boys and girls at the rural level using English as the medium of instruction. The school views primary education as a major stepping stone towards social mobility, equality and employment opportunities. Since its inception, the school has been committed to encouraging education for girls. From being the first English-medium school in Bali to admit girls to being recognized as one of the five Changemaker Schools in India in 2018 by Centre for Science and Environment (CSE), the 25-year celebrations of The Fabindia School in 2017 were indeed a celebration of 'My Good School'.

The 'My Good School' designation shows the value a school places on professional learning and student achievement.

The school works for the personal and social development of an individual, by subscribing to our philosophy of quality in education, offering an environment where experiential learning is made possible through activities beyond just study; this brings to life learning that would otherwise be theoretical and uncoordinated.

Four children, as depicted in the logo, are at work in school, and as a community, build the My Good School.

Education = Service + Skill + Sport + Study

The colours of the My Good School are symbolic of the underlying philosophy. The collaborative magenta for Service, symbolizes young people who bring the world together and do not like being differentiated on the basis of colour, caste, creed or other divisive ways. Communities must be built. The serene green for Skill is used as the word green is closely related to the Old English verb 'growan', to grow. Individuals must develop skills for life. The electric cyan for Sport affirms that we cannot make any colour without this primary shade, which portrays the need for a 'basic' understanding of the needs of the young people. The royal blue for Study is all-pervading and the dominant colour. It enhances vision—we need to think 'beyond the blue' and that intellectual development is a necessity.

My Good School helps young people follow their passion in Service, Skill, Sport and Study. The four disciplines form the key elements for delivering quality education. The school may focus on one as their speciality, but a good school works to deliver a balance of all. Every person for us is a full 10/10. What matters is the emphasis we as individuals give to each of the four S's. For some, 'Study' could be a full 10, for some it could be 'Sport', yet the most complete individuals will value each of the four S's and find themselves.

My Good School works for the personal and social development of an individual by offering an environment where:

- Experiential learning is made possible through activities beyond just study, and this brings to life 'learning' which would otherwise be theoretical and uncoordinated.
- By encouraging students to become involved in activities in the community outside the confines of the school curriculum we would help develop their confidence, knowledge and networks.
- With teachers encouraging young people, the students can benefit from what the school and outside interests have to offer. This can be a key factor in their progress from adolescence into a fulfilling and rewarding adult life.

For me in particular, the quest for My Good School continues and the journey so far has brought a great sense of fulfilment.

The credit for this must go to The Doon School and the great masters who have not only reshaped our lives but have even set the benchmark for quality education in India.

A country is as developed as its education sector. We in India should make 'affordable quality education' our development mantra and this alone will help us develop as a great nation. No matter what path we take on the road to economic development, the speed-breaker will always be the quality of education!

Foreword

Sandeep is a passionate educator. He is one of those individuals who have dedicated his life to making the greatest impact to the greatest number of people. The way he has chosen to do that is by helping schools and teachers implement programs that will help students to become lifelong learners.

He believes in the idea that if you can change a child's life, you can change the life of their family, their community and indeed their nation. He has lived up to his motto for the last 35 years of his life in helping teachers improve their skills, helping school administrators understand how to deliver the best learning outcomes, helping school heads foster communities of curiosity, openness, learning and creativity in their schools.

Sandeep has taken his lifelong experiences and summarized them in this thoughtful, provocative and very readable book.

I have had the pleasure of watching Sandeep's work in the school I founded 30 years ago and the proof of his work lies in watching the graduates of the school who came from a small rural community do extraordinary things with their life.

He has shown that regardless of where one is born, one's social or economic status, a good school can transform a child's life by helping them learn and develop into ethical responsible global citizens.

This book explains how schools can achieve significantly

better teaching standards, foster a sense of community and help each student reach their fullest potential.

Sandeep does a great job of framing the issues that educators, school owners and administrators face, and also where they must focus their energy. As he said at the beginning of Chapter 2, 'A country is as developed as its Education sector. We in India should make "affordable quality education" our development mantra and this alone will help us thrive as a great nation. No matter what path we take on the road to economic development, the quality of education will always be a speed breaker.'

Sandeep's book is an invaluable read for policy makers, school owners, administrators and teachers as it takes a 360-degree view of all aspects of what it takes to build great schools. The emphasis he places on the development of a strong culture of teacher's training is reminiscent of Henry Adam, who said, 'A teacher affects eternity and one can never tell where their influence stops.'

Applying the ideas in this book will transform how schools can deliver outstanding learning outcomes. I can say this as I have watched Sandeep apply this idea at The Fabindia School over the last 10 years as Chairman of the board.

Sandeep is able to do this successfully as he is a lifelong student. I hope you enjoy this book as much as I did.

William Nanda Bissell
Chairman of the Board, Fabindia

Introduction

I come across many people who say they own a tract of land and would like to set up a school. But should just owning land be enough to consider setting up a school? Some say they are promoting a township and must set up a school. Yet others have real estate and find running a school to be a great revenue-generation proposition.

Is the school a good way to earn social acceptance, a way to espouse philanthropy? The challenge is not in owning or setting up a school, but operating it well and delivering quality education. We need to understand the purpose of the school before we set out to build it with brick and mortar.

A school is where students (or 'pupils') are taught by teachers. Most countries have systems of formal education, wherein students move through a series of schools. The names for these schools vary by country, but generally include primary school for young children and secondary school for teenagers who have completed primary education. An institution where higher education is taught is commonly called a college or university.

Mr Shomie Das, a renowned educationist and former headmaster of The Doon School and of Lawrence School, Sanawar, says:

The term education encompasses a whole gamut of experiential learning which, in a school, is given through teachers in the classroom and often, more importantly, outside. It is the nature of the experience and how it is designed to be imparted that makes the difference between a good school and an ordinary school. How are the academic subjects taught and what is it a school should teach? There are three important functions, among others, of the educational process in the classroom apart from mere learning:

- To develop problem-solving abilities
- To develop creative abilities
- To develop curiosity and an inquisitive spirit

Does the school have systems of teaching and learning that encourage the development of the aforementioned skills? What place does the library have in the learning process? In the assessment systems used by the school, how much emphasis is given to marks?

Often the opportunities for learning outside the classroom are greater, through sports and games and other activities like adventure sports, dramatics and community service. They all play an important role in developing character and citizenship. A good school will provide a balance of opportunities in its curriculum to allow a student to develop his or her special interests and talents.[1]

---

[1] Dutt, S. (2007). *Guide to Good Schools of India: the top residential schools in India* (7th ed.). The English Book Depot.

So, we must put a lot of thought before we set out to build a school. It is imperative to understand that we are moulding the lives of our future generation.

When a potter starts his work with clay, he has his mind and body in unison and strives to build a piece of art and utility with empathy, care and devotion. He does not make the pot simply because there is mud that happens to have the properties of high quality clay, which when sold will earn him his livelihood. The potter's labour of love is what really goes into the making of a masterpiece. Likewise, many an artist has a canvas to paint; few, however, can imbibe the thought and emotion to create the depth that will be endless.

Our advice to all owners of real estate and property developers is: once you start to work on a school project, you will need to forget all other work in your life, put your heart and soul into this very project and then alone can you create a school to offer quality education.

Please do not simply consider your investment in setting up a school, as a business decision. The challenge lies in the operations, and the effort involved towards ensuring the personal and social development of a child is humongous. Training people to deliver the promised quality is never an easy task.

Quality in education consists of happy teachers, a good student-teacher ratio, modern equipment and adequate space and classroom facilities. A good school should offer facilities for retraining teachers and good salaries at par with related spheres. A well-designed school should have modern aids and teaching devices. A school should be a centre for excellence. It should employ good teachers and pay them well. It should encourage a concern for the environment and cleanliness. Above all, it should be managed by a dynamic principal and competent, humane teachers.

Successful people are punctual and ensure that they deliver the quality they promise. If you have land, you have a long way ahead for setting up a school with quality commitment which is not going to be an easy task. There are many buildings that exist with no students and have dilapidated campuses. Many dreams turn sour simply because the schools do not have the right leadership.

Leadership Matters

A campus alone is not a school. It needs people with compassion and values who will help deliver quality education and will help the entrepreneur maintain quality. If you want to make a good school, it is important to find people with compassion and passion, for then alone will your land become the ideal place for fertile minds. Innovation lies in building and growing and not simply in sowing and forgetting. If you have a piece of land and other infrastructure, you will need to partner with the community, the people and the society to help build a good school.

The school must be in the best hands and often it is the principal who makes the difference. The role of the principal covers many different areas, including leadership, teacher evaluation, student discipline and community relations. Being an effective principal is hard work and time-consuming. A good principal knows how to balance various roles and responsibilities while keeping abreast with the changing trends in education.

So if you have land, you need the best principal and, in principle, you are often not the best principal for the dream school! The owner must simply be a mere resource-provider and entrust the principal with the freedom to lead and to make it an institution. People make the place and they alone can shape lives. Children are tender not only in body but more so in heart and mind.

A.N. Dar, former principal of Scindia School, states,

> The challenge with promoters, they need to give space to people they entrust the school to...teachers are there but they need to be respected—and trusted—and given time, recognition and encouragement. Many well-known schools are floundering because the school is not giving them the space required by them. There are appraisals and increments and even sacking but the quality of staff is not growing.

Teachers and the system must show a balance so that the soul of the school is retained.

Having a Vision and a Mission

The most important feature of a transforming organization is that it has a 'vision'—or what I would like to call the school's desired future. We have to make the school an important societal change agent for the future, to bring about any transformation in learning and social development in any community or country.

First and foremost, we must list what a school vision must be:

- The vision must be initiated by the leader and developed with school personnel and all stakeholders.
- It must provide future orientation.
- It must set an overarching direction.
- It must evoke an image of the future school.
- It must provide a standard of excellence, an ideal.
- Is the vision, the basis for the unique contribution to students, to school personnel, community and society?
- The vision should be shared and supported by the internal and external stakeholders.
- The vision must be compelling and inspiring.
- Finally, the vision must be living and even evolve further as the process of change creation rolls out.

Steve Jobs said, 'Innovation requires a team, and you cannot inspire a team of passionate evangelists without a compelling vision; a vision that is bold, simple and consistently communicated.'

A book that has contributed immensely to my learning is *Schools Can Change: A Step-by-Step Change Creation System for Building Innovative Schools and Increasing Student Learning* by Dale W. Lick, Karl H. Clauset and Carlene U. Murphy. That, and my understanding of the work of Learning Forward, the professional learning association for educators, helped me to crystallize a vision statement for The Fabindia School: 'The Fabindia School will become a national leader in innovation by implementing new technologies in learning and offer affordable quality education.' Another way to state the school vision could be, 'The Fabindia School will become a national leader in schools and become the favoured destination for English learning in rural India.' The first statement is compelling and inspiring, the second seems to me a statement of purpose, and explains to all the stakeholders what is in it for them. This perhaps is our goal and is indeed a part of our vision wherein we have set out to become an institution of excellence, and there is an element of dynamism in what we are doing. The vision thus sustains over an extended period of time and is the direction for the ongoing mission.

A study by Bain and Company[2] indicated that organizations that have clearly defined vision and mission statements aligned with a strategic plan outperform those who do not.

A mission statement does the following:

- Defines the present state or purpose of an organization;
- Answers three questions about why an organization exists: **WHAT** it does; **WHO** it does it for; and **HOW** it does what it does.

It is important to develop a plan around a clearly defined and well written vision and mission. Both serve important, yet different roles as core elements of a strategic plan. Again taking the example of The Fabindia School, its mission is to provide access to high-quality education for boys and girls at the rural level, using English as the medium of instruction. The school views primary education as a major stepping stone towards social mobility, equality and employment opportunities.

The vision must encourage us to think big (overview), think for tomorrow, think of student and society contribution and most importantly lead and help to create the future:

---

[2]Discover Journals, Books & Case Studies, Emerald Insight. Retrieved on 20 June 2020, from https://www.emerald.com/Insight/viewContentItem.do;jsessionid=86F49424FD0A254DA690C9732E383FC2

learning for staff and children; motivate them and win them over with a bright future; team up and deliver.

Vision killers are often tradition, being risk-averse, stereotypes, complacency and short-sightedness. We must not look for quick results and look at details to help create the big picture.

The vision must be cognitive–to educate; emotional–to motivate; and organizational–to coordinate. An effective vision produces more efficient and coordinated action. It must be coherent, powerful, emphasize on what is achievable and always clarify what the school should be.

Vision without action is a dream. Action without vision is a pass time. A vision must be a shared one as this alone will make it become a reality one day.

Taking a School from Good to Great

Elements that make a school good are: good systems, great training and a scholarship programme.

At the core of any vibrant society or any institution we need systems to manage, ensure deliverables and achieve our goals. No game can be won without strategy and this is the key to success. Today we have tools and good professional help to put in place systems to build a good school. It's critical to understand the connection between good people and good systems. Good systems support good performance and drive good outcomes. Systems represent best practices which allow good people to excel. They provide consistency and predictability, eliminate waste and guesswork, and free people up to perform at their best. Schools must be better managed and the resources optimally used to help deliver 'affordable quality education'.

The greatest systems, technology, and ideas in isolation won't transform an organization at all levels. Change creation for building innovative schooling and increasing student learning, is possible only if we manage our schools better. We need to put in place best practices and transform the leadership of the institution. To make this possible we need right people, find the right place and do the right job. To put in place this system we need great training. We must not confuse systems with technology or IT as we often do. A system is a good process that makes efficient delivery possible. Yes, technology is an enabler and a mere tool, it is not a solution.

Training is the key to building the best staff team. With the changing times, we have to continuously align our growth and development to meet the changing needs of the people, the society and the economy. A learning organization brings to life an ecosystem for intellectual growth and development of the young people. We need to move from competition to collaboration and today the students too have a lot to add to our professional growth and development. The challenge for us is to first connect, then communicate, go on to collaborate and finally create. Knowledge is the epitome of creation. We need to have the best faculty to put in place the most fertile learning environment. To make this happen we have to continuously train and retrain to help deliver the growing aspirations of our people. Teachers today have to be regarded as professionals, like doctors, lawyers and managers. They need to keep learning and building up their professional capabilities.

To make education meaningful, it must be inclusive and

we need to value each and every individual for his/ her ability and needs. This is only possible if we have a good scholarship programme. Expanding the outreach of a school, is the area of social concern, a scholarship programme to promote the educational interests of both the needy and the deserving students and thus helping them in shaping their careers helps make the world a better place. For youth to meaningfully grow and be a part of a harmonious society, we need an egalitarian economic model, to equip one and all with quality education. The power of knowledge can not only transform minds but help build sustainable livelihoods.

Right from ancient times where wisdom or knowledge was not subject to patients or selfish wealth creation, we have examples of how the haves and have-nots work together in the conquest of knowledge. Education without boundaries is best achieved if we make it available to all without fear and favour. The power of knowledge to help transform lives is well established and is the only path for better livelihood for one and all.

Another thing that cannot be stressed enough is that schools must be havens for personal freedom. Nobel laureate Rabindranath Tagore has very beautifully eulogized freedom at school in his poem 'Where the mind is without fear'. The poem is read as a prayer in many schools and for me personally this is the 'haven of freedom' a school should be.

Overall, schools are one of the safest places where children can be. However, some schools have problems, such as bullying and theft, which make them less secure. These problems make students and educators feel less safe, and it makes it harder for students to learn and for teachers to do their jobs. There are still bigger challenges. The world has been shaken up with the brute violence like shootings in school, Boko Haram kidnappings, killing of innocent children by violence and design. Traditionally we looked at school safety for ensuring our children were 'accident safe' and that their journey to school was safe too. Today the monster of terrorism and the brutal design of radicals have threatened the school space even more. The fear psychosis will not only push us to take recourse to policing and security, but more than that will need counselling and great efforts to soothe the terror-stricken minds of the children of the world.

In the times that we live in, it is imperative for every school to have crisis teams that review their plans regularly and staff members who greet and challenge every person who comes to the door. They should have locked doors, safety drills and parents who know where to find their kids, just in case the unthinkable happens.

According to Ken Trump, President of National School Safety and Security Services, schools need counsellors, psychologists and officers building relationships with kids, because they are the best line of defence.[3]

What is most important is that schools work to prevent problems through community building, fostering respect, inclusion, fairness and equity.

---

[3] *Parents and school safety*. (13 April 2017). School Security. Retrieved on June 30, 2020, from https://www.schoolsecurity.org/resource/parents-and-school-safety/

This book is not the result of my theoretical views; it is steeped in my decades-long association with schools, working closely on various aspects to ensure we help them deliver better. When we work with schools, our focus is creating an environment where:

- Experiential learning is made possible through activities beyond just study, which can consolidate and bring to life learning which would otherwise be theoretical and uncoordinated.
- Encouraging students to involve themselves in activities in the community outside the confines of the school curriculum will help develop their confidence, knowledge and contacts.

Quality in school education consists of happy teachers, a good student–teacher ratio, modern equipment, adequate space and classroom facilities. A good school brings together the parents, students, teachers and the management to partner for the personal and social development of the child.

I hope this book helps you realize the importance for every child to have the My Good School experience in life and also discover the role that we can play in helping create such schools.

SECTION I

THE WHAT, THE WHY AND THE HOW OF TEACHING

Why Go to School?

There is a universal movement to send all children to school. I wonder if that is the only way to provide them with an education.

What is education? Isn't it liberation with responsibility? If we look back at how things were, say, a thousand years ago, we realize that schools weren't the only means of providing an education. To promote schooling as a universal solution is like working on an assembly line. One may even see in it the seeds of cloning! Are we trying to 'mass produce' identical individuals by sending them to school? One may argue that the aim is to offer every person equal opportunity, freedom and liberty to lead a respectable life. But the question is: does the existing 'process' provide that? The literacy vs education debate is never-ending and, as is often the case, the so-called education we provide only works for universal literacy.

The 'School of Life' is an environment for an individual to bloom and find oneself, and this is the real school that we need. A school that we all are pushed to attend is not a substitute for it. A school is not a venue or a building, but an environment. It is not an escape from the misgivings of life, but a haven of opportunity. More often than not, present-day schools are not places we should go to. The Nobel laureate Desmond Tutu had said, 'Inclusive, good-quality education is a foundation for dynamic and equitable societies.'[1] This line really is the inherent philosophy that schools must abide by. Most schools, due to economic necessity and societal bias, skirt the main reason as to why we should go to school. According to the American politician Roy Barnes, what is most crucial is that schools recognize that it is the needs of the students that must be at the centre of the system. He says, 'But the fact is, no matter how good the teacher, how small the class, or how focused on quality education the school may be, none of this matters if we ignore the individual needs of our students.'[2]

In the words of researchers Max Roser and Esteban Ortiz-Ospina, 'A school is an educational institution designed to provide learning spaces and learning environments for the teaching of students (or pupils) under the direction of teachers. Most countries have systems of formal education, which is commonly compulsory.'[3] When there is a compulsion, are we not curbing freedom? Realists will question the need for absolute freedom and counter that a process and environment of delivery are essential. Looking back, we find that education, the way it is delivered in schools, has created economic imbalances, strained the ecosystem and added to many inherent challenges. Some even go on to say that science, the panacea of all evils, has also created its own demons. No

---

[1] Tutu, D & Roekel, D.V. (25 May 2011). *Facing the future: Global education at the crossroads*. HuffPost. Retrieved June 11, 2020 from, https://www.huffpost.com/entry/facing-the-future-global_b_544449

[2] Roy Barnes Quotes. BrainyQuote.com. Retrieved 20 June 2020, from https://www.brainyquote.com/quotes/roy_barnes_246362

[3] Roser, M & Ortiz-Ospina, E. (2013). *Primary and Secondary Education*. Our World in Education. Retrieved 30 June 2020, from https://ourworldindata.org/primary-and-secondary-education

system is perfect, and thus all of us going to the same school and not finding ourselves is really an anomaly.

The school denotes a learning environment, it should not be identified as just a physical space, as we have today come to describe our places of learning. The ancient philosophy of learning was indeed far superior to our modern school methodology of 'by hearting' practised at most schools. Open mindedness and tolerance, in all forms, should be encouraged so that curiosity and the desire to experiment increases. Physical, psychomotor, emotional, intellectual and spiritual training can be accomplished with a pragmatic approach. One can only make improvements in the scheme through trial and error, and learning from others' experiences.

Why go to school? The question itself is a challenge but we need to reflect on what kind of school rather than the need for going to school. Perhaps the most distinguished learners, as well as great people, have often not cared to go to school, the place we are all being forced to go. What we need to attend is the 'School of Life'. The learning or, in fact, the curiosity within is the best fire to ignite and that needs a good environment, not just a process as employed by most schools. The 'School of Life' is made up of family, peers, nature, the world around and historically the need for human beings to live in harmony.

I believe the question 'Why go to school?' will remain unanswered forever, and what can be called a school is a debate in itself. If we can help individuals think, learn and find themselves, the journey through school will be a rewarding one.

Quality in Education

A country is as developed as its Education sector. We in India should make 'affordable quality education' our development mantra and this alone will help us thrive as a great nation. No matter what path we take on the road to economic development, the quality of education will always be a speed breaker.

We have public schools, independent schools and government-aided schools. To provide an all-round education, it is best to be financially independent and beyond the pale of direct government control, to be free to innovate and keep education alive. There are Nursery Schools, Primary Schools, Secondary Schools and Senior Secondary Schools. Day Schools tend to load the homework on students and are still not ideal. Boarding schools offer a good learning experience and usually admit children starting at the age of about 10 onwards, and have a capacity of 500 plus students.

There are 52 State Education Boards and two National Education Boards in India. The Central Board of Secondary Education (CBSE) is limited, as it eliminates international exams as additional streams. The Council for the Indian School Certificate Examinations (CISCE) is an autonomous body and it is more in tune with freedom for innovation. For international recognition, it is feasible to consider additional streams, such as the British 'O' levels and 'A' levels and the International Baccalaureate (IB).

The quality in education consists of happy teachers, a good student-teacher ratio, modern equipment, adequate space and classroom facilities. A good school should offer facilities for retraining teachers and fair salaries at par with related spheres, such as those of white-collar workers in the healthcare and legal sectors. A well-designed school should have modern aids and teaching devices. A school should be a centre for excellence. It should employ motivated teachers and pay them well. It should encourage a concern for the environment and cleanliness. Above all, it should be managed by a dynamic principal and a team of competent, humane teachers. Schools should not be teaching shops being run solely for commercial gains. Teachers should be well read and inspired people.

The teachers should read about education, love the children they teach and have well-rounded personalities. They should acquaint themselves with the Montessori methods, the philosophy of Swami Vivekananda and read John Dewey, Rabindranath Tagore and Jean Jacques Rousseau. Quality in education leads to quality in our lives and that is what we are all striving for.

The last few years for me, in particular, have been of the greatest learning as I moved from the high-flying job of the National Director of The Duke of Edinburgh's International Award to what was made for me—the Chairman of the Bhadrajun Artisans Trust. Away from the city lights and located in the village of Bali in Rajasthan, at the foot of the Aravali range, the trust runs The Fabindia School with a mission to provide access to high-quality education for boys and girls at the rural level using English as the medium of instruction. The school views primary education as a major stepping-stone towards social mobility, equality and employment opportunities. Since its inception, the school has been committed to encouraging education for girls in a culture where most parents who can afford an English-medium school for their children would send only their sons.

Outward-bound and experiential learning triggered a rush of adrenaline in me and thanks to my long-standing friend and Chairman and Managing Director of Fabindia William N. Bissell, I found what I love to do the most in life—being with children in the outdoors. While life in Bali village has indeed been slow-moving and quite uneventful for many, for us it has been a drive in the fast lane as we have been trying to find the true meaning of 'quality in education' and deliver this at an affordable price.

With a dedicated leadership team and staff committed to making dreams come true, our school today really is a 'piece of land brought to life'. It is most heartening to share the learnings from The Fabindia School and to write that we have found the road to affordable quality education. This has widened our horizon and we believe that education for sustainable development is the need of the hour.

According to UNESCO, the lead agency for the UN Decade of Education for Sustainable Development,

> Education for Sustainable Development allows every human being to acquire the knowledge, skills, attitudes and values necessary to shape a sustainable future. Education for Sustainable Development means including key sustainable development issues into teaching and

learning; for example, climate change, disaster risk reduction, biodiversity, poverty reduction and sustainable consumption. It also requires participatory teaching and learning methods that motivate and empower learners to change their behaviour and take action for sustainable development. Education for Sustainable Development consequently promotes competencies like critical thinking, imagining future scenarios and making decisions in a collaborative way. Education for Sustainable Development requires far-reaching changes in the way education is often practised today.[4]

Personal and social development of an individual forms the core of affordable quality education:

- The experiential learning, possible through activities beyond just study, can consolidate and bring to life learning which would otherwise be theoretical and uncoordinated.
- Encouraging students to become involved in activities in the community outside the confines of the school curriculum will help develop their confidence, knowledge and contacts to follow their passion after they leave school. This will greatly enhance the opportunities for their personal and social development.
- With teachers encouraging young people, they can benefit fully from what both the school and outside

---

[4]*What is ESD?* | *United Nations Educational, Scientific and Cultural Organization.* UNESCO | Building peace in the minds of men and women. Retrieved June 11, 2020, from https://www.unesco.org/new/en/unesco-world-conference-on-esd-2014/resources/what-is-esd/

interests can offer. This can be a key factor in their successful progress through adolescence into a rewarding and fulfilling adult life.

What is the prescription for schools to deliver affordable quality education? Our experiences show that there are some major steps needed to do this, some of which are listed here:

- Focus on skills that build employability.
- Ensure teachers are groomed to be leaders and mentors.
- The senior management must be trained to deliver better.
- The parents and the community are equal stakeholders in the school's operations.
- Need to use the latest technology and updated curriculum.
- English proficiency and better communication skills.

From our learnings in the education sector, we feel that some of the challenges are to:

- Use the existing curriculum to deliver better.
- Assist young people to identify and plan their challenges.
- Support young people in enhancing their skills.
- Work within operational and administrative challenges.
- Find an available opportunity for youth in the community.
- Build relationships at different levels.
- Empower young people to find themselves.

Affordable quality education must have four key elements built into the curriculum: Service, Skill, Sport and Study. This provides the roadmap for the personal and social development of an individual. The children must learn about themselves, their relationships with other children and adults, both within and beyond the family. The concepts of fairness and justice must be introduced and children should be encouraged to think about and respect the feelings of others. The importance of motivation, perseverance, self-esteem and a positive disposition to learning, all have a significant role to play in children's learning and development.

I see the possibility of a nation where every school offers young people the opportunity to be rewarded for challenging themselves, for engaging with adult mentors, and for giving back to their communities after finishing school. I believe we can change their world when we help connect young people with new opportunities.

How Your Child Learns the Best

In an educational setting, an analysis of the student's learning needs helps them identify where they are in terms of their knowledge, skills and competencies, versus where they wish to be, that is, what their learning goals are.

In the words of Rhonda Wynne of Learner Centred Methodologies, Ireland, students learn better when they can see a reason or relevance as to why they are following a programme of study. By conducting a learning needs analysis with prospective students, the learning provider can identify what programs are needed. Including learners from the outset will help ensure that course content, schedules, etc., are in line with the needs of the student. By assisting the learner to identify the gaps in his/her own learning, the provider will be better able to support the student."[5] A learning needs analysis will help:

- Identify what skills and knowledge the learners already have.
- Highlight skills/knowledge/competencies that need developing.

---

[5]*Learner Methodologies*. Asset Project Info. Retrieved 30 June 2020, from http://www.assetproject.info/learner_methodologies/before/characteristics.htm

- Identify clearly what students wish to achieve.
- Outline and define expectations and goals.
- Establish need and demand for the course.
- Determine what can realistically be achieved given the available resources.
- Identify any obstacles or difficulties which may arise.
- Increase the sense of ownership and involvement of the students.
- Provide information about the student group—know your audience.
- Achieve a correct fit between the provider and the student, i.e. the course matches student needs and expectations.
- Identify the content that best suits the student's needs.
- Determine what is the most appropriate delivery format—class-based, online or a mix of these and other formats.
- Determine what skill set and knowledge-base is required of the tutor.
- Develop a budget and cost-benefit analysis.
- Establish what is the most suitable time to deliver the programme and over what timeframe.
- Ascertain the most suitable evaluation mechanisms.
- Outline what results can be expected and if/how these can be measured.

According to Antonise Crawford of the Village Preparatory School, Cleveland, 'Teachers plant seeds of knowledge that grow forever.'[6] Just as a number of factors are needed for the

---

[6] Crawford, A. *Teachers Plant Seeds of Knowledge that Grow Forever PowerPoint.*

seed to flower in a garden, our students too need much more than simply the right environment to flower. We as mentors need to first map the needs of each child, as each of us is different and it is said that no two people in the world are alike. The biggest challenge in helping a child to learn is thus, in taking the right steps to help him/her to grow not only in mind and body, but in heart and soul too. Complete education is only possible if we know what the true needs of the students are. There is no 'one size fits all' when it comes to a curriculum. The teaching methods are what matter and not only the content forced on to the students. The methodology must fit the needs of the individual student.

At a very early age, our current system of education starts working like an assembly line, and the curriculum rolls out the 'one size fits all' approach. This is where the inherent challenge lies. Continuous learning will only happen when we can identify the students needs. The only constant is change, and the needs also go through catalysis and this makes the challenge even bigger. The needs of the students push us to explore new vistas of learning—service, skill, sport and study all offer us avenues to find out what the student needs. Once we have the interest of the student at the core of learning, we will be able to see a quantum leap in learning and will empower the seed of knowledge to develop into holistic learning. The needs of the parents, teachers and all stakeholders will have to supplement the needs of the student alone and not vice versa. There are different forms of learning delivery and in

---

(8 December 2012) Share and Discover Knowledge on SlideShare. Retrieved 10 July 2020, from https://www.slideshare.net/neecee12/teachers-plant-seeds-of-knowledge-that-grow-forever-powerpoint

most schools, the mentor is the one who leads the learning process. What we need to do is offer the lead to the student, with the mentor in a supportive role.

There are several questions that the parents must ask while evaluating a good school for their child. A non-exhaustive checklist of such questions is given below[7]:

- Teacher-student ratio (total strength of school, number of teaching and non-teaching staff, class size)
- Quality of teachers (Qualifications, experience, levels of motivation, training and development undertaken, competency)
- Academic and administrative support available to the teachers
- Access of staff to contemporary research and development and pedagogic trends
- Curriculum design (academic and co-curricular activities)
- Hobbies, sports and spare time activities
- Involvement of every student in different aspects of the curriculum
- Academic options available to students

Does the school offer the opportunity for experiential learning? The best of learning is only possible when we see that the facility to ensure experiential learning is inbuilt in the school design. The school is a piece of land brought to life—a land with freedom, opportunity, joy and space for each individual to find

---

[7]Dutt, S. My Good School. Retrieved 10 July 2020, from https://www.goodschools.in/

herself/himself. How should parents choose among the array of schools available? Should they opt for an old, established school? Should they instead try out a new, innovative school? Is a day school better for their child and their family, or a residential one? What kind of fees should they expect to pay for what kinds of facilities? Is a co-educational school suited to them or a single-sex school? The list of questions is infinite; the answer lies in one challenge and that is to identify the students' needs. This is truly the first and last point of call for each parent/mentor.

It is imperative for us to understand that the students' needs will change over time, and we should not become complacent on our part. Learning itself has a level of dynamism and energy to it, and this should propel us even further towards our goal of building knowledge and competence in what we love to do. The first and the final steps will always be the students' needs, and not the simple timetable set by the school, or the curriculum set by the education department of any state. The state, the school and the society have often not understood the needs of the students. The economics of the process, the cost-effectiveness of delivery of education and the needs of the industry and the nation may direct us to deliver education in one way, and this is where the real challenge lies.

Don't Be Afraid to Fail[8]

> You've failed many times, although you may not remember.
> You fell down the first time you tried to walk.
> You almost drowned the first time you tried to swim, didn't you?
> Did you hit the ball the first time you swung the bat?
> Heavy hitters, the ones who hit the most home runs, also fail to strike out a lot.
> R.H. Macy failed seven times before his store in New York caught on.
> English Novelist John Creasey got 753 rejection slips before he published 564 books.
> Babe Ruth struck out 1330 times, but he also hit 774 home runs.
> Don't worry about FAILURE. Worry about the chances you miss when you don't even try.

There is opportunity in self-learning, collaborative learning, online learning and today, informal learning is finding its proponents. The methodology is not the question, it is the objective that matters the most, and the bull's eye is 'identifying the students' needs'. No effort should ever be spared to help the individual seed flower in the garden of knowledge and the world of opportunity.

---

[8]United Technologies Corporation (1981). *Don't Be Afraid to Fail* [Advertisement]. Wall Street Journal.

Performance Scores Must Be Honest

Performance in a class is defined as a figure or letter representing the total number of marks awarded in an examination or competition, and signifies a person's score. Marks must be true and that for us is the biggest challenge today.

In our quest to encourage the student to perform or show that we as teachers are delivering better, and to build the brand of the school where parents feel their students are delivering better, the marking system is used and, dare I say, abused. Now, we have a system where we do not wish to hold back or fail a student and deny them promotion to the next class. The merit list is made only from performance scores. Yet, schools and colleges often fail to spot budding talent. Are the performance scores/marks the only way to help an individual deliver? Are they a true measure of the capacity and capability of the student?

What Is Beyond 100 per cent Marks?

When we motivate students by giving marks or scores for their performance, we also end up harming those who are given low scores. The losers in the marking system are perhaps many more than the winners. Yes, you are justified in saying that we do need a system/measure to judge performance, and marks are one such way to measure the learning outcome in the individual. It is imperative that we look at the sanctity of the system and not get carried away by the simple need to win over people with false promises. During my travels and meetings with school heads, I had the opportunity to speak with one such educationist who was particularly honest in saying, 'We have to give marks to keep parents happy; if we are strict with marking, the student scores fall, parents then feel that the school is not delivering!'

We have now gone a step ahead and have started publishing dubious listings and performance ladders for schools. The annual listing, the much-awaited media hype and sensationalism is all harming the education process, rather than helping it. Good work itself outshines the 'good word' sold to us by media hype. We may come to the top-of-the-mind recall by using the annual media listings. However, like a newspaper, the value of these listings is very short lived. At the end of the day, it is good work that will lay the foundation of growth and development of young people with character. Today, it seems to be 'business first'. Like the yawning gap between the haves and have nots, the alleged meritocracy is killing learning and doing more harm as it is often clouded with a business motive.

A traumatized parent asked, 'Some schools are liberal in giving marks while others are not. Will I not suffer on account of strict marking by my child's school?' The hypothetical answer to this question is: no student would suffer because of strict marking or benefit from lenient marking as the marking scheme for all question papers in all major subjects is being provided by the Board and the teachers are being directed to adhere to this marking scheme. However, to avoid such apprehensions, the CBSE has also undertaken a systematic collection, analysis and moderation of 'Evidence of Assessment' by analysing sample answers scripts, anecdotal records, student portfolios and teachers' records. This exercise ensures that school-based assessment is of acceptable quality.

Like the CBSE, the other national and state boards too have a policy and use various methods to correct the bias, if any. To err is human, and this is the anomaly and the challenge in itself. Whether the method of providing grades instead of marks is a better way can be one of those never-ending debates. What is imperative is that the assessment method should not be prone to mere individual value judgements.

The National Foundation of Education Research tries to explain 'What do test scores mean?'

Many people will remember test scores from their school days such as '7 out of 10' for a primary school spelling test, or '63 per cent' for one of their secondary school exams. Such scores are readily understandable and are useful in indicating what proportion of the total marks a person has gained, but these scores do not account for factors such as how hard the test is, where a person stands in relation to other people, and the margin of error in the test score. As another example, in a school test such as Mathematics or English, we would not know how well the pupil is performing against National Curriculum measures.

Standardized scores are more useful measures than raw scores (the number of questions answered correctly) and there are reasons why such scores are normally used. The measure of the spread of scores is called the 'standard deviation' and this is usually set for educational attainment and ability tests, and for many other tests. This means that, irrespective of the difficulty of the test, the students are given marks on a rationalized scale. This may help correct the individual bias in marking and is often preferred by the national and state level boards. Further the practice of external examiners, the random testing, the other secure methods all aim to remove the human bias.[9]

While marks may be a means to encourage competition, they could also dampen the spirits of low scoring students. The teacher must carefully consider the method adopted and ensure that the marking is honest, if this be the only way to measure the performance of an individual. There are countless stories of individuals who get poor performance scores, but go on to succeed in life, become inventors, innovators and bring about a revolution in thought. The human mind is very complex, and this performance measure is the biggest challenge and will remain one always.

Another interesting debate asks 'Should Student Test Scores Be Used to Evaluate Teachers?'[10]

How much to credit—and blame—teachers for student performance is an issue that continues to confound the education field. To what extent is each student's progress directly attributable to the teacher's efforts? What other factors

---

[9]NFER. *An Introduction to Standardised Scores*. Retrieved 30 June 2020, from https://www.nfer.ac.uk/for-schools/free-resources-advice/assessment-hub/introduction-to-assessment/an-introduction-to-standardised-scores

[10]*Should student test scores be used to evaluate teachers?* (24 June 2012). WSJ. Retrieved 11 June 2020, from https://www.wsj.com/articles/SB10001424052702304723304577366023832205042

can determine a student's success? Is there a way to measure each factor separately, including the teacher's influence?

To clarify: We should focus on gains in test scores, not end-of-year scores. Any estimate of how much the student has improved while in the teacher's class must take into account the fact that students start at different points. We want to know how much a teacher contributes to student growth during the time students are in that teacher's classroom.

While such student-achievement gains are imperfect measures, the same is true of all measures. The marks given by the teacher are sacrosanct and are perceived as the ultimate reflection of a student's ability. (It is most important that the teacher be accountable and that their ability be reflected in the child's performance.) Perhaps the answer lies in giving due weightage to the performance of an individual as well as the ability of the teacher to bring about an improvement in the quality of learning, and not just a measure of teaching efficiency in a classroom. If a teacher delivers a lesson and the child is supposed to comprehend, then I am sure both play an important role and will influence the final marks in the class.

The Centre of Learning and Teaching, Iowa State University has published an interesting read on 'Classroom Assessment Techniques'.[11] The simple way of assessing a person with marks is not the best method, but is widely used as it is the most practical and teachers per se are supposed to have the moral authority to deliver the value judgement.

---

[11]*Classroom assessment techniques*. Center for Excellence in Learning and Teaching, Iowa State University. Retrieved 11 June 2020, from https://www.celt.iastate.edu/teaching/assessment-and-evaluation/classroom-assessment-techniques-quick-strategies-to-check-student-learning-in-class

If marks are the evidence of assessment, these must be transparent and this is where we as teachers need to be very careful.

When marking an assignment or test, we are often influenced by several factors: the pressure of time, the inability to comprehend the answer the student wishes to convey, the environment around us and even our mental makeup on the day of corrections!

We must reflect and do our best to be most honest. The performance mark must be used judiciously to convey a message to the student and to the family that puts in everything to help the child grow and succeed in life.

As Deepika Tandon, former principal of The Fabindia School, Bali, Rajasthan, puts it succinctly,

> This is the struggle of today's system. Everyone thinks he/she is an educationist. But no one bothers to bring the enjoyment of learning to their students. The curse comes from the Appraisals attached to money rather than appreciation in terms of recognition. Marks have a way to build certain documents for schools, but they tie us up in knots when it comes to following a methodology of awarding them.
>
> CBSE has taught me one thing via corrections and that is to be at the child's side when it comes to correction. If we can come down to their level of teaching we should come down to their level of correction too.
>
> Continuous Assessments are actually the bane because they have warped people's thinking. Objectivity is a far cry and teachers end up being confused rather

than being clear because they are not left on their own to decide how to judge!

I agree with you that the marking system produces more losers than winners. Thank you for taking such pains to reveal the ugly as well as the fairer side of the system.

Performance scores must be used as a true motivator and not a mere measure. The joy of learning and succeeding must not be robbed in the process of marking. Yes, it is a great feeling to top a class. But it is only one person who will top, and is that the only way to run the race of life?

We must not simply see the scores at one point of time, but over a period of time and this is where we will find value and be able to develop a strategy to build individual performance. Value judgements in life are indeed clouded with bias and it is time the sanctity of the system is maintained. The real teacher alone will stand to help the student progress in life, far beyond just gaining high marks in a classroom. This will help make up for the lack of belief we have in the integrity of the performance scores.

People, Process and Outcomes

Effective change will only come about when we have the right leadership and put in place a process to achieve our outcomes. Schools can change and this is only possible when we have a change sponsor or change agent. The next step, of course, is the target of change and how we advocate this. There will be a continuous need for the same people to play different roles as circumstances change.

How Do We Bring about the Change?

There are some things that we can do to bring about change.

- Leaders must become aware of the concepts of limited assimilation capacities of individuals.
- Before we set out a new project, involving major change, a thorough analysis of all existing projects should be undertaken.
- Projects should be prioritized.
- All but the highest-priority projects should be considered for termination or reduction in scope.
- A plan should be developed and implemented to eliminate and reduce scope of lower-priority projects.

For teachers to deliver change in the school process, we have to make our priority list and ensure we are realistic in the projected outcomes. A process is only as good as the people who deliver it. Effective sponsorship of change in schools needs significant commitment.

According to Learning Forward, the professional learning association, 'Leaders throughout the pre-K12 education community recognize effective personal learning as a key strategy for supporting significant school and school system improvements to increase results for all students. Whether they lead from classrooms, schools, school systems, technical assistance agencies, professional associations, universities or public agencies, leaders develop their own and others' capacity to learn and lead professional learning, advocate for it, provide support systems, and distribute leadership and responsibility for its effectiveness and results.'[12]

To overcome resistance to change, we must win over teachers, and this is only possible when, as trainers and managers, we are able to explain to them that the school is simply an ecosystem for their personal and professional development. When we look at the most successful schools, we find they succeed only because they have a 'teachers first' policy. This is akin to the retail mantra of 'employees first'. Most people often have a short-term view and are reserved at the outcome of any process. It should be made very clear that the outcome of the change will indeed be their personal and professional development.

A good school must have a 'people first' philosophy,

---

[12] *Leadership*. 24 September 2019. Learning Forward. Retrieved 20 June 2020, from https://learningforward.org/standards/leadership

and any organization is as good as the people they have. No amount of money spent on infrastructure will be able to build an efficient process, unless we work to train and develop a strong staff team. Every school must have a Teachers' Centre for professional learning and development. Only when the school becomes the best training institution will it achieve the outcomes of delivering quality education. The schools sector has to look at the hospitality and medical sectors for their innovative ways and means to serve the community better. In the hospitality industry, on-the-job training is the key to better delivery. The Hyatt way or the Taj way of delivering experience and learning are good examples of a 'people first' approach. These organizations work very hard to raise the bar for their staff to deliver and offer customers delight. Similarly, we need to make sure that all teachers—new recruits as well as those already in classrooms—are well-trained, have access to ongoing training and are treated as professionals, with decent pay and conditions. It is important to recognise and acknowledge that:

- Without teachers, a school is just a building.
- Without trained teachers, schooling is not education.
- Without trained teachers for all, education for all will never be a reality.

For the best outcomes, we have to look at schools as training grounds for teachers and ensure they are looked after very well. There are many examples of successful schools, where nearly 70 per cent of the school operating cost is the amount paid as teacher salary and the cost of training and development. To have the best people, beyond just training we must value them as an invaluable resource too. I sometimes get carried away and say, at the risk of being misunderstood for calling humans robots, that 'a good school is like a teacher factory'. This is indeed true and the emphasis is on the fact that most leading schools work to empower their staff, and a school like The Doon School, Dehradun takes pride in the fact that after a few successful years in the institution, their teachers go out as vice principals and leaders of other institutions. The school process has to be thorough and must deliver to the aspirations of those employed by the school; we must note it is happy people that make a better institution. For the process to deliver the outcomes, it is the people alone who can do it.

People, Process and Technology work to create the ecosystem of high quality delivery, and we must have a 'people first' policy in all schools and educational institutions. For a country to develop, it is the quality of schooling that must improve, and this is only possible by having the best of people and processes to deliver our outcome.

The role of people and process matters a great deal as this relationship reflects in the quality of work. Our efforts to improve quality will often reveal that handling both people or process for change simultaneously, can be an arduous task.

It is worth asking, 'Should I manage the people or manage the process?' We must make sure we think about both. We should gauge which are genuine issues and which are misleading ones before we make a decision. We inhabit a space where people, process and technology come together to create innovative solutions for schools. It would be impossible to do what we do without the brilliant minds working tirelessly behind the scenes.

The Human Face of Change

In dealing with the natural human reactions inherent in school change, says Robert Evans, a Massachusetts psychologist and school consultant, leaders would benefit from orienting their efforts not around techniques but around a few key predispositions or biases[13]:

- Clarity and focus
- Recognition
- Participation without paralysis
- Confronting entrenched resisters

We know that effective teacher training is essential. Providing the school staff with leadership positions and opportunities to grow their careers in education is the best way to ensure better outcomes from our process. As a business model, schools work to create cash surplus for development and expansion. This often makes them cut the budget for human resources and staff training. Low wages will yield low returns, and thus, the desired outcome will never be achieved. Schools need to not only hire good people, but also offer them the best environment for their personal and professional development. The school business must be sustainable and work towards the personal and social development of a student. This will only be possible when we adopt a 'people first' policy and ensure that the people who run the process are not only well looked after but enjoy the work they do. It is often said that the right people at the right place alone will deliver heart-warming service and process delivery.

---

[13]Cushman, K. (11 October 1997). *The Human Face of Change*. Coalition of Essential Schools. Retrieved 30 June 2020, from https://essentialschools.org/horace-issues/the-human-face-of-change

Choice of Curriculum

In ancient times, India had the Gurukula system of education in which anyone who wished to study would go to a teacher's (guru) house and request to be taught. If accepted as a student by the guru, he would then stay there with the guru and help in all the household activities. This not only created a strong bond between the teacher and the student, but also taught the student everything about running a house. The guru taught everything the child wanted to learn—from Sanskrit and the holy scriptures, to mathematics and metaphysics. The student stayed as long as he wished or until the guru felt that he had taught everything he could teach. All learning was closely linked to nature and to life, and not confined to memorizing pieces of information.

The modern school system, including the learning of the English language, was originally brought to India by Lord Thomas Babington Macaulay in the 1830s. The curriculum was restricted to 'modern' subjects such as science and mathematics, and subjects like metaphysics and philosophy were considered unnecessary. Teaching was confined to classrooms and the link with nature was broken, so was the close relationship between the teacher and the student.

The central board and most state boards currently follow the '10+2+3' pattern of education and will move to the

'5+3+3+4' system as per the New Education Policy 2020. In the existing pattern, 12 years of study is done in schools or in colleges, and then three years of undergraduate education for a bachelor's degree. The first 10 years are further subdivided into five years of primary education, three years of upper primary, followed by two years of high school.

The National Council of Educational Research and Training (NCERT) is the apex body for curriculum-related matters for school education in India. It provides support and technical assistance to a number of schools in India and oversees many aspects of enforcement of education policies. Other bodies governing the school education system are:

- The state government boards, in which the majority of Indian children are enrolled.
- The CBSE, which conducts two examinations, namely, the All India Secondary School Examination (AISSE—Class/Grade 10) and the All India Senior School Certificate Examination (AISSCE—Class/Grade 12).
- The CISCE, which conducts three examinations, namely, the Indian Certificate of Secondary Education (ICSE—Class/Grade 10), The Indian School Certificate (ISC—Class/Grade 12) and the Certificate in Vocational Education (CVE—Class/Grade 12).
- The National Institute of Open Schooling (NIOS) conducts two examinations, namely, Secondary Examination and Senior Secondary Examination (All India) and some courses in Vocational Education.
- International schools affiliated to the IB programme and/or the Cambridge International Examinations.
- Islamic madrasa schools, whose boards are controlled

by local state governments, or are autonomous or are affiliated to Darul Uloom Deoband.
- Autonomous schools like Woodstock School, The Sri Aurobindo International Centre of Education Puducherry, Auroville, Patha Bhavan and Ananda Marga Gurukula.

Additionally, the National University of Educational Planning and Administration (NUEPA) and the National Council for Teacher Education (NCTE) are responsible for the management of the education system and teacher accreditation.

The structure and institutional change proposed by the New Education Policy 2020 will start unfolding in 2023 and we will need to wait for another 10 to 15 years to see any significant changes.

School Boards Compete for Better Academics

Several city schools are switching from Secondary School Certificate (SSC) to ICSE, to IB Programme and/or the Cambridge International Examinations, citing 'excessive meddling' by the state's education department as the reason. Meanwhile, the CBSE is offering new subjects and courses for its students and is also promising 'no bag and no homework' to primary students. ICSE, too, has been making similar announcements over the last few years. I would like to share some observations and views of heads of schools, as reported by Times News Network (TNN)[14]:

---

[14]Srivastava, R. (26, February 2004). *Test of boards: ICSE scores over SSC, CBSE, Mumbai news, The Times of India*. Retrieved 10 July 2020, from

Curriculum

Most academicians believe that the SSC board syllabus is 'textbook oriented,' while ICSE has a 'wider outlook for all-round development of students,' says Nandita Jhaveri, vice principal of New Era High School, Panchgani. According to her, the ICSE curriculum has more practical applications than both CBSE and SSC. Educationist Kavita Anand adds that schools affiliated to ICSE have the liberty to choose from a large variety of books and authors available in the market for their students, whereas CBSE and SSC schools have to stick to books issued by the board. Some years back, *The Times of India* carried this news and the TNN news service caught up with educationists all over the country to solicit their views.

Quality/Relevance of Textbooks

According to school principals, SSC textbooks have remained unchanged over several years, whereas ICSE books are more relevant to contemporary times. CBSE updates textbooks every year as part of its 'frontline curriculum'. '10 per cent of irrelevant or outdated material is replaced with more pertinent matter,' says Vrinda Malse, principal of Naval Public School, Mumbai.

Exams and Evaluation

'In ICSE, students are evaluated in a variety of ways through the year. For instance, 20 marks are allotted for project work,' says

---

https://timesofindia.indiatimes.com/city/mumbai/Test-of-boards-ICSE-scores-over-SSC-CBSE/articleshow/520196.cms

Jhaveri. SSC still encourages rote learning and the test papers are essentially based on textbooks. Thus, 'qualitative evaluation of children as done by ICSE and to some extent by CBSE, is not possible with SSC,' says Ramakant Pandey, principal of Bansidhar Agarwal School, Mumbai. ICSE also scores on popularity charts among educationists, as it encourages students to do research and 'get into the habit of finding out and not just learning'.

Extracurricular Activities

CBSE has a well-networked state and national-level sports activity set, according to Malse. While SSC schools cannot recruit teachers for such activities, ICSE gives a free hand to schools to recruit trained teachers.

School Affiliation

CBSE	Central Board of Secondary Education
SSC	State Secondary Board
CISCE	Council for the Indian School Certificate Examination
IB	International Baccalaureate
IGCSE	International General Certificate Examination, U.K.
(X)	Class 10
(XII)	Class 12
(A)	A Level, equivalent to Class 12

A Comparative Study of CISCE and CBSE

	CISCE	**CBSE**
Medium	English	English or Hindi
Pattern	10+2+3	10+2+3
Pass Mark	35 per cent in each subject in ICSE 40 per cent in each subject in ISC	33 per cent in each subject
Books	• Allows schools to select textbooks except for languages and other resource material. • Defines Scope of Syllabus.	NCERT books
Candidates	Only Regular candidates are permitted to take the examination. Private candidates not permitted.	Regular and Private candidates permitted.
Course of Study	Education aimed at enabling students to acquire comprehensive knowledge leading to enhanced performance in competitive examinations.	Examination-based Curriculum
Assessment	Has an effective evaluation which adapts to external changes (Flexible)	Has a traditional exam pattern (Rigid)

Please note: This is a very abbreviated and objective comparison. There is a growing list of subjects offered by the two boards. Parents, while selecting schools, should be aware of the Board Examinations, their scope, limitations and their differences. Further information can be retrieved from the respective offices.

The choice of a school curriculum further adds to the agony of parents choosing a school for their children. Beyond plain simple economics and the way the Boards compete to market themselves, the parents and guardians are often influenced by peer pressure and by the fancy of the children themselves. At the secondary level, the choice of a school probably looms large in a child's mind too. He or she may have firm opinions, perhaps based on where their friends are going. Parents and children must discuss it together. Try to get the child thinking in terms of his or her own needs, which may be quite different from someone else's. Talk to the child's teachers. They will have much to contribute and will be able to make certain recommendations. However, they cannot make the decision for the child. Begin by considering these simple questions:

- What are the child's academic abilities?
- What is the child interested in?
- What are the things the child is particularly good at?
- What are the things the child struggles with?

Schools for me are temples of learning; only when we look up to this great place with due regard and purity will we ever develop as a nation. I wish I could visit a school every day and be with children as they truly make life more meaningful for all of us. As the best of our growing years are spent in a school, the choice of the school curriculum is even more important than the physical infrastructure and the geographic affinity. We pay for the services and the facilities; the school curriculum is standard and duly prescribed. The learning environment thus matters even more. The schools that work to deliver the curriculum with a 'child first' philosophy are more successful and capture the imagination of many parents.

CBSE vs ICSE

Often parents are confused between CBSE and ICSE. Which board to choose? What are the differences between CBSE and ICSE? Which board will be better for the development of the student? These and many other questions haunt the parents. You will find here the most comprehensive set of answers to these questions.

Spread or Prevalence

The CBSE board is the more popular of the two by a huge margin. It is followed in 18,000+ schools in India and abroad, thereby making it easier to find schools when you move to a new city.

Schools Outside India

Here CBSE takes the cake over ICSE (CISCE). CBSE schools, titled CBSE Videsh, can be found in the Middle East, South Africa and even in some European countries. So, you can move countries without significant disruption of education for your kid.

Recognition by Colleges in India

Both the boards are recognized by most universities and colleges across India. So, marks for Class 12 will be recognized.

Phew! That is one less thing to worry about. However, some colleges have started the process of 'calibration' of marks. This means they put an adjustment factor for marks obtained in one board to make it comparable to the other. This calibration factor often varies from year to year and usually favours the board with the greatest number of applicants, which in this case is the CBSE.

Course Content

Both CBSE and ICSE (CISCE) have slightly different focus in terms of course content. The CBSE content is more focused on Science and Maths with more attention paid to application of knowledge. CISCE (ICSE), on the other hand, is more balanced with equal focus on language, arts and science. The latter is my personal preference. While I would want a more balanced curriculum for my child, it is up to what you prefer.

Teaching Methodology

Both CBSE and ICSE (CISCE) prescribe a certain teaching approach and both have undergone significant change over the past 10 years. Generally, the focus has increased on learning through experience and experimentation rather than through one-way teaching. This is for the better! Ultimately the quality of instruction depends upon the school and less on the board. There is not much to choose here.

Freedom and Flexibility

ICSE (CISCE) prevails over CBSE here. There are a lot more subjects to choose from in Class 12. Also, there is an option to take vocational courses based on interest rather than pure academic courses for Class 12. CBSE has been improving over the years in terms of combination of subjects offered, but ICSE still has a lead.

The focus should be on effective learning, which happens if the learning is active and if it is enjoyable for the student. Active learning, i.e. learning by doing (vs passive listening or watching) helps a child retain up to 45 times more. Further, if they enjoy the learning process or outcome, then their interest and understanding increases manifold. Schools and teachers have to make special efforts to achieve these twin objectives of learning—active and enjoyable!

In the words of Peter McLaughlin, former headmaster, The Doon School, 'Young people are looking for clear leadership at the national and international level from the adults in society, but see a woeful lack of intelligent, decisive and ethical leadership in practice. We should teach boys and girls the theoretical foundations of influential leadership, and how to make the calculated and informed decisions that are required to make a positive difference in the world.' This is what most of the established curriculum has not been able to achieve. The curriculum needs to be supplemented with experiential learning at all levels. Education is to be filled with dynamism that helps us meet the aspirations of the young people.

Today we have schools that follow international curriculum and market themselves as offering quality education at a premium price. What is most important here are the teachers they employ. The choice of the board does not necessarily make a school better or even good as per the expensive marketing campaigns. What matters most is the quality of teachers and the training they have in rolling out the curriculum. Ensure you have the best mentoring for your child, and the choice of the board, though limited, will not be the key differentiator. Please list your priorities and make learning most enjoyable for the child.

Building Schools with Quality

The key to good education delivery is in the hands of the teachers. Thus, the first and foremost need of a good school is to have a Teacher Development Programme. It is imperative that schools invest in teacher training as their number one priority. We need heart and soul, and not just brick and mortar to make a great school. Teachers are the most important asset of any good school, and there is a need to help them, empower them and give them the best for their career development. When teachers enter a school, their first goal is their career. Today, this is an important need a management with vision must fulfil. A school that offers good training will have a lower attrition rate, and this in turn will help offer better education. Please note there is enough evidence to show that it is not money alone that makes people happy.

Good systems and effective use of technology is another way to help schools build quality. Teaching and learning is made fun with audio, video and digital delivery. We can make the classroom an exciting and stimulating place. In addition, we must use IT (Information Technology) to help deliver better processes. When we put in place good processes and systems, the work environment will improve; there will be more accountability and better time management. Schools involve a lot of administrative work and this makes the life of the teacher, the management, the parents and, more so, the students difficult. Reports, record keeping, accounting and transport management all make running the school a complex exercise. We now have reasonably priced solutions and school management software and learning management systems, which make life easier for all at school. Find the best solution and deliver better with good systems.

The third important element is the Scholarship Programme in a school. Education is only complete if it is inclusive, secular and affordable. We can only build a nation by having good schools that bring together children and young people from all communities and groups aboard one ship. When in uniform, all children may look the same, but it is imperative that a school accepts children not only on the ability to pay the fee but with a larger motive of laying the foundation of a great nation. The success of institutions the world over rests on the ability to find the best talent. To build the brand of the school, there is a solid need for having a well-run scholarship programme. The awarding of scholarships must be done by partnering with the community and should be need, as well, as merit based. First need and then merit, since it is often the challenge of going to school that comes before the challenge of building a meritocracy.

Training, having efficient systems and scholarships are the three key elements for quality delivery in a good school. From high-end modern city schools to rural schools, all need to move from good to great and this will only happen when we embed the three winning elements in the vision and mission of the school.

For school culture to thrive the three most important

qualities are Diversity, Inclusion and Belonging. **Diversity** improves tolerance, empathy and critical thinking. **Inclusion** or Inclusive education provides a friendly atmosphere which helps in empowering students and Staff. **Belonging** is acceptance and pride of the Institution. These strong feelings build up confidence and belief, and help build schools with quality.

Fun in Learning, Learning Is Fun

Fun is the beginning of anything fundamental. Even the first three letters of the word 'fun-da-mental' spell 'fun'! For anything to be mentally stimulating, 'fun' must be the essential ingredient. This is how learning begins and ends. The day you miss out the 'fun' element in education delivery, learning will come to an end. For beginners at school, the teachers' biggest challenge is how to make learning fun.

It is often said that there is a child in each one of us and only the young at heart understand that fun is an essential element of any learning process. As trainers, teachers, mentors and peers, we often find that we are pushed and taught, but this is not really the best way. There is a need to 'pull' with fun and this makes learning effective. The use of colour, sound, touch, smell and taste is the first step to make learning effective. In our kindergarten years our teachers have to act, perform and do all manner of wild things to hold our imagination. The Montessori method of teaching aims for the fullest possible development of the whole child, ultimately preparing them for life's many rich experiences. Montessori teachers are trained facilitators in the classroom, always ready to assist and direct. Their purpose is to stimulate the child's enthusiasm for learning and to guide it, without interfering with the child's natural desire to self-teach and become independent. Each child works through their individual cycle of activities and learns to truly understand according to their own unique needs and capabilities.

Stimulation is the key to excite the mind to learn and enquire freely. We must go beyond the basic five sensory approach in our learning environment and help develop the fertile young mind with games and discover the true self within. Good teachers know how to go beyond the five senses. What constitutes a sense is itself a matter of some debate. We are taught that we have only the five senses of touch, taste, smell, hearing and sight to guide us. It turns out that we have been underestimating ourselves. Scientists count between 14 and 20 actual senses, such as perception of pressure, heat and pain, and interoceptive senses like that of balance, most of which aren't taught in primary school. It is important to see what information we are really working with and what it will take to make learning fun.

Fun must be the process and not necessarily the objective of teaching, as sometimes fun and frolic make us go off on tangents too. For a teacher, the challenge is to have the energy to go on-and-on and have fun too. Ask any teacher and I am sure they will say that the classroom environment and delivery of a curriculum often set a tedium—boring, monotonous, dull, uninteresting, unexciting—and this is the true test for building a great learning environment. Very few are gifted with the ability to innovate endlessly, and it is just these individuals who are the best teachers and make learning fun.

For most people, the teacher at the kindergarten level is their introduction to the learning and education process. Many will never forget their first teacher, and this is simply because there is more fun at the start of the teaching process in any school. We will always need to be more creative to keep alive the early childhood years and help us live with the child within.

Life Is Parenting

The parent community looks at the school as a factory. They send raw material and expect a great product rolled out! The reality of the matter is that the school is only an ecosystem and all the stakeholders must work together to build a nurturing learning environment. What parents and guardians do at home has a greater impact on children than what they do at school. Teachers are expected to work hard while children get away with all the mischief, and parents play the blame game.

In the words of the American writer Brian Tracy, 'If you raise your children to feel that they can accomplish any goal or task they decide upon, you will have succeeded as a parent and you will have given your children the greatest of all blessings.'[15]

I must re-emphasize that what parents and guardians do at home matters much more than what the children do at school. With three decades of parenting to back me and over 30 years of work volunteering with the schools and leading young people, I emphatically state, 'Life is Parenting'. We are born with empathy to nurture our young ones with kindness and care. The cycle of birth and rebirth, as some would say,

---

[15]*Brian Tracy quotes*. BrainyQuote. Retrieved 20 June 2020, from https://www.brainyquote.com/quotes/brian_tracy_125750

tempts me to say parenting is infinite. Children, for their parents, never grow up!

Life is the school from which we will never graduate, and learning is the fun that makes life worth it. Parents must find time and be intrinsically involved and grow up with the children. Many of us in our quest for economic comfort, will say that today as both the mother and father have to be bread earners, they do their bit to give a better world to their children. I am sure the biggest investment you need to make is time, as this alone will fulfil all the emotional needs of a child and will even make up for any material shortfall. The first and last teacher will be the parent alone.

US Senator Joe Manchin has said, 'Every child should have a caring adult in their lives. And that's not always a biological parent or family member. It may be a friend or neighbour. Oftentimes it is a teacher.'[16]

Parenting (or child rearing) is the process of promoting and supporting the physical, emotional, social and intellectual development of a child from infancy to adulthood. Parenting refers to the aspects of raising a child aside from the biological relationship.[17]

Pat Kozyra, educator and author of *Tips and Tidbits*, suggests that we must have routines and consistency for our children, for ourselves and even for our pets. Routines and consistency are so important for helping a child cope up with getting ready for school, doing the assigned homework and learning to be organized. If this means putting up a check list

---

[16]Joe Manchin quotes. BrainyQuote. Retrieved 20 June 2020, from https://www.brainyquote.com/quotes/joe_manchin_168545

[17]Brooks, J. B. *The Process of Parenting* (9th ed.) (2012). McGraw-Hill.

for our children and ourselves, then by all means we should make the priority list. An example is putting the child in-charge of getting the school bag ready the night before so that he or she knows what is in it and what is not. Teachers get so tired of hearing, 'My mother or my helper didn't put it in there, I guess,' or 'I forgot it at home,' or 'I don't know where it is.' We must appreciate that our child should know where their things for school are, and surely morning is not the time to struggle.

Kozyra goes on to say that homework should always be done at a desk, with proper lighting and writing instruments, away from the TV and the many electronic gadgets that have today invaded our lives. The noise level in the house should be monitored, and homework should not be left until the child is too tired or ready for bed. That is just too late!

Parents want their child to read, to concentrate and may even want them to speak in English, but do they do the same? When I was young, my mother would sit down with us when we did our homework; she was our Wikipedia and Google, our anchor and our conscience keeper. With her knitting and crochet in one hand, and eyes set on us, she gave us the luxury of the best mentorship. Find me a mother in this day and age, without a gadget in her hands when in the company of her young ones—it will be a challenge. Not many fathers will read aloud to their children today, and rarely do we have the luxury of grandma's tales either. Yet, we call ourselves good parents and find the schools guilty of letting us down when we see our child lagging in the class. My father with the qualification of a 10th class pass was my best handwriting teacher, and my mother a postgraduate in Sanskrit taught me how to speak correctly, have the best etiquette and above all be a team player. Most of our parents did not have the qualifications we have, but their knowledge and the fire in them to learn and be the best parents, made them our best teachers.

We must find time to simply be with our children in peace and comfort, and give them the most precious gift of time. I believe that if we invest in our children, we will be rewarded with peace and well-being and will enjoy the never-ending flow of parenting.

An Eager Child or Enthusiastic Teacher?

Some of the things one often hears in the parent and teacher meetings and at other forums are: 'This child is not interested,' or, 'The child should show some curiosity or interest in the subject,' or, 'The child is not attentive in the class and does not keep up with his or her work.'

Most often the burden to learn is put on the child by the teacher and the parents. On the opposite end of the spectrum are teachers who are so enthusiastic that they do not have disinterested students in their class! What, thus, is essential to having a great classroom experience? If I asked you to name your favourite teachers from kindergarten through graduate school, it would be easy to answer, wouldn't it?

In the words of Professor Richard Leblanc, an award-winning teacher at York University, Ontario, 'Good teaching is as much about passion as it is about reason. It's about caring for your craft, having a passion for it, and conveying that passion to everyone, most importantly to your students.'[18]

Fun begets fun, if the teacher is enjoying their work, certainly the students will love the process of learning. Having a good time is human nature, and students to yearn for good

---

[18]Leblanc, R. 'Good Teaching: The Top Ten Requirements'. (1998). *The Teaching Professor*, Vol. 12, ed. 6.

times. Hard work and dedication do not mean that we cannot have fun. As a teacher I can say with conviction that the more effort I put in, the more my students have fun and experience the joy of learning. Having a class full of fun, does not mean that it is all fun and games either and that no teaching or learning will happen. This simply shows us that the teacher enjoys their work and this translates into a better classroom environment. Teaching as a profession calls for hard work and fun to go together hand-in-hand.

Having Fun while Working Hard

There are other words that are similar to enthusiasm and passion. They also describe our favourite teachers. Here are a few of them[19]:

zest	excitement	energy	fervour
eagerness	enjoyment	delight	zeal
liveliness	vitality	vigour	devotion

Teachers have many challenges in their teaching careers, but the most important of all is the need to motivate students, how do you handle the unmotivated students and, above all, build an environment for every child to learn and grow.

Different methods of teaching are needed to motivate students and improve their understanding. This is possible only when the teachers show a lot of patience and perseverance.

---

[19] *Lesson #1: Good teachers share one special quality.* Catholic Education Resource Center. Retrieved 20 June 20202, from https://www.catholiceducation.org/en/education/catholic-contributions/lesson-1-good-teachers-share-one-special-quality.html

An unmotivated student needs to be welcomed into the classroom and an environment created to help the student achieve great things. There is the need to encourage the unmotivated student to participate in the class; this can be done with activities, doing question and answer sessions and not insisting on the right or wrong answers. They must feel that the classroom is a safe and interesting place, and that even giving wrong answers is just okay.

The teacher must never be critical, instead work to increase a student's self-esteem by rewarding positive and good behaviour. They must continue rewarding the unmotivated students for their good deeds. This will encourage them to behave positively.

Extra effort must be put in with the unmotivated students; the teacher needs to build a good relationship with the students, talk to them about life and their future. Sharing of life experiences and the mistakes a teacher makes or encounters in life, offer interesting learning experiences for the students.

While teaching, a teacher needs to be enthusiastic and maintain a high level of energy. Giving small and positive challenges to unmotivated students helps them build confidence. There is a pressing need to teach them how to face an unfavourable situation and allow them to evaluate and monitor themselves.

Learning beyond accumulating knowledge is the most enjoyable activity, and this is where the onus of making the classroom experience engaging lies on the teacher. Most of our teachers are pushed into the profession by chance and not by choice. This is the reason why so many educators do not have any fun in the classroom and treat teaching as a process.

It all begins with fun! Fundamental begins with 'fun', but it also has 'mental' in it. Any form of learning must begin with fun and then move to the mental ability. I explain this as fun with mental ability to get the true meaning of fundamental. I hope the linguists will not censure me for this rather overt interpretation. The teachers' quest for learning and stereotypical thinking will pose a challenge when they connect with young people. Only if fun is meant for all will there be any form of creative learning.

Today we talk of learning beyond the classroom, we literally need to move out of the four walls of the room and stand beneath the open sky; without our creative ability we will not be able to infuse the fun element in learning. All sociologists and even most educationists rely on life skills to initiate learning and education. The key element of life skills is 'fun' alone, and this has been the proven and tested method for working with beginners and adults. We rely on icebreakers, mind games, brainstorming, all enforcing the hypothesis that it is 'fun' that makes it happen. It is imperative for us as mentors to engage with youth and never miss out the fun.

Many students leave school only able to think in words, a limited and un-dynamic way of thought. But even worse for them, the 'Joy of Life' that comes from creative thought is lost. Ideas of the visual dimensions of the brain including mathematics must make it the most beautiful object we can possess in the universe. Our minds are by far the greatest mechanism we can ever possess and yet we hardly take notice of it. It is, as Tagore writes in 'Parting Words', our 'playhouse of infinite forms'.[20] This is the marvellous choice we can make in life. The greatest and the most beautiful mind.

Let us not be escapist by pushing the burden on the student. It is really the leadership of the teacher that matters and ignites the mind of the eager learner. Before a good 'shishya', there must be a good 'guru', and often it is said we follow in the footsteps of our mentors. In the words of the students, the 'boring' teacher is the one who is not able to recognize the eager child. Yes, it is important to be eager and this preludes the enthusiasm that propels us to further learning. For a great classroom experience we need the eager teacher and the enthusiastic child. A teacher must be an 'eager beaver', defined as one who is exceptionally, often excessively industrious or zealous. Beavers, considered to be extremely industrious, are always building dams. A teacher too can be eager and industrious, just like the beaver.

O my great teacher if **you** want to work in a great place, find a great leader—or become one yourself. The leader is within you and the choice is yours to delve within, enjoy what you do, have fun and lead the students to a great learning experience, and not once should you ever complain that the student is not eager to learn. If you as a teacher enjoy your job, the students will love every minute of your class and you will have every student be the eager child.

---

[20] *Rabindranath Tagore Gitanjali* 'When I go from hence'. Tagoreweb - The Complete Works of Rabindranath Tagore. Retrieved 22 June 2020 https://www.tagoreweb.in/Verses/gitanjali-190/when-i-go-from-hence-2911

Why Teachers Are Averse to Change

For any school to develop or for that matter, for any organization to grow, change-management is the most daunting task. Teachers are the real agents of change, and only when they take the onus of leading the change will it reflect in a school. No system or school management can succeed without first addressing the challenge of handling the reservations our teachers have.

Over the years, the education curriculum at schools has not undergone significant change and has not really kept pace with the modern-day innovation needs. The teachers have become too comfortable in what they have been doing for years and some may say they do not want to 'sweat it out'. To be the change, one must first change oneself, and this is what innovation is all about. Many of our teachers are doing the job more as a profession of chance and not a profession of choice. There are very few people for whom teaching would be the first choice of profession. This is where the real challenge lies: today our guru does not stand on the pedestal where our history and culture portrayed them. Likewise, the student is not really in awe of the teacher, and this is because his/her needs are not met by the education system. The biggest challenge for us is to make teachers feel appreciated, and make teaching the most sought-after profession in the nation.

Teachers have a reason to be averse to change, as they find themselves on the receiving end from all the stakeholders in the education process—the parents, the students, the management; even society as a whole is not really as appreciative of our teachers and their work. This lack of appreciation leads to loss of self-esteem. The urge to live in the age of consumerism leaves little scope to be innovators, free thinkers and learners. To top it all, the outdated syllabus and the tools of delivery all make their job most uninteresting. Further, in most cases the students outdo the teachers in terms of lifestyle and earning capacity, and this makes the teacher even more pessimistic in outlook. Some find being 'once a teacher, always a teacher' makes them quite staid and even brings about a feeling of isolation. These teachers become victims of their own circumstances, as they believe their destiny is to be stuck in the profession alone.

Many use teaching as a way to pass time as they study, pursue other academic programmes and prepare to get better jobs. For them teaching is only a small earning venture for a limited period of time, a stopgap arrangement before they move to other things. This is a fallacy as many then end up trying for years to move out, but do not make it. They end up not giving their best in the class and end up following the same lesson plan, the same way all their lives. Only when they see that every student has the potential of being an Einstein and that they alone can find the genius in every child, will they value their profession and go on to innovate.

With limited time and resources and the huge demand for schooling, we get away with poor quality delivery in any school. This is perhaps another reason for sub-standard teaching and why we get away with our teachers living in denial of the fact that they need to study and improve throughout their lives. Teaching is a profession with no entry barrier and teachers have the most onerous task of building young minds; this is not the best environment for academic delivery. Low wages, lack of knowledge, no teaching standards and, most of all, the never-ending population pressure for schooling make teachers quite pessimistic in their outlook, and averse to change.

For any nation to grow, teachers must be the changemakers and should not resist change. They will have to go beyond the self, and like soldiers work selflessly as always and help young minds grow to develop into great teachers! The need of the hour for administrators, governments and policymakers is to work towards making teaching the most sought-after profession. This alone will help us overcome the teachers' aversion to change and help us reach our full potential.

SECTION II

REDEFINING EDUCATION AND LEARNING

Reading at the Heart of Education

It is said that 'by reading we read' and this is true. We also learn to write by writing; the more practice children get, the better they become. After all, as the classic saying goes, 'Practice makes a man perfect!'

With persistence, one can climb the toughest rockface with just a rope, similarly with practice the brain can decode any complexity. Reading is a proven method for brain building. If you read you improve your learning ability; today when attention spans are being reduced to split seconds, the ability to read and comprehend tends to get lost.

Having had the honour and privilege of running one of India's premier bookstores, there is not a day when I have not had a parent or an individual requesting me to guide them to enable their child to start reading books. Reading is the heart of education, the knowledge of almost every subject in school flows from reading. One must be able to read the word problems in maths to understand it. If one cannot read the science or social studies chapter, one cannot answer the questions at the end of the chapter. The computer manual which is essential to its operation may be complicated, but it must be read. Reading is arguably the single most important social factor in any society.

Room to Read, a non-profit organization promoting girls'

education and literacy in Asia and Africa notes: 'When a book is good, people want to talk about it. Therefore, bookstores themselves are social spaces.'[21] Pat Kozyra further goes on to say, 'the more you read, the more you know; the more you know the smarter you grow; the smarter you are, the longer you stay in school; the longer you stay in school, the more qualified you become and this will then lead to a better earning and a better life.'[22]

In today's world of technology though, enjoying reading is losing its charm with students. They have lost the patience to relax and read, empower their minds with knowledge. It is for this reason that The Fabindia School started a programme called DEAR (Drop Everything And Read). This activity is carried out in all the classes under the guidance of the principal herself and works to enhance the reading ability of the students. It takes place every Monday, right after Assembly, for 20 minutes. Teachers and students are expected to sit and read either their favourite book or story or even read the newspaper. It is compulsory for everyone to read during this time of the week.

Ms Deepika Tandon, the former principal of The Fabindia School, states,

> Students looked hesitant initially on the first Monday; but after two Mondays, this was seen as a tool to help improve the school's campus language! From compulsion

---

[21]RoomtoRead. (2 October 2014). *When a book*. Twitter. Retrieved June 30, 2020, from https://twitter.com/RoomtoRead/status/517474100789641216

[22]Kozyra, P. (2013). *Tips and tidbits for parents and teachers: Celebrating 50 years in the classroom and sharing what I have learned*. Strategic Book Publishing.

to necessity [is] often a way to find a solution, and this precisely we need to do to encourage reading. DEAR is a way to increase vocabulary; improve pronunciations; be able to read better and increase one's comprehension.

When we read a book, our mind moves from real life to reel life; we start visualizing and this is the first step to any form of learning. There are certain things that parents can do at home to help their child to read:

- Become a good reading role model for your child. Let your child see you reading something every day. The child is likely to ape the parent's behaviour, and we have to be cautious of what we practise and not simply keep preaching.
- Some families set aside a family reading time each day when the TV and cell phones are off and everyone is reading something, no matter what the age.
- Make a variety of reading materials available at home.
- It is never too early to get your child interested in the newspaper.
- Subscribe to a family magazine or several children's magazines.
- Start a family library and add 10 books for each member each year.
- Better still, when you go shopping, you may have the option to drop off your child at the nearby bookstore/library, giving them the perfect opportunity to simply browse.
- Be encouraging and praise the child's effort to read; do not keep pointing out errors.

- Read to your child every day. Some experts say, 'Do not stop reading to your child until he or she is in university!'
- Read bedtime stories.
- Have books in the car.
- Take books to appointments to read while waiting.
- Read books while relaxing in the park.
- Hook the child on to a series and make them collect books of one author or theme.
- Label objects around your home to help your child learn a sight vocabulary.
- Whenever you look around, wherever you will see the written word—signboards, directions, name plates—keep observing and absorbing.

The list of suggestions and things-to-do is endless; we simply have to make it a habit and enjoy it. All children and adolescents must have access to quality books, no matter what their race, economic status or capabilities. Reading inspires confidence, bridges the differences between people, and forms a fundamental stepping-stone to better communication skills. We believe it is the single most important skill a child can develop to become a productive member of society. Books open children's minds to a world of possibilities, while stimulating their intellect, imagination and intelligence, especially during their formative years.

Storytelling is one of the best methods to encourage reading. Tales and folklore have long been the most interesting way for us to communicate across generations. Most of our stories today are available in the printed book form. Our movies are based on books, and what a picture conveys is powerful too. At school or at home, it is most wonderful to have a teacher, parent or a peer enthral us with stories and insight. This will then encourage the young people to read too, as they too should be made to do some storytelling as an activity.

Read to lead, supplement the reading habit with regular library visits and maybe even research projects. Another step ahead could be that the students are asked to prepare or read up some material before attending a scheduled class. They may then be asked to explain the lesson and even supplement the teacher's effort to deliver the learning in the classroom. When we give the students a chance at leadership, we help them become better learners and readers.

We need to set up a book club or a library society that is run by the students and let them manage the school library as well as help their peers find what is interesting to read. This will ensure the library is well stocked with books the young people want to read and will have them visit the library too. This may need some guidance and supervision of adults or an experienced teacher or an individual who is well read and well informed. The school may even arrange for the students to visit the nearest bookstore, accompanied with the school staff, when library books are purchased. Care should be taken to not stock the library with leftover books or material that is donated and irrelevant for the needs of the students.

As we sum up, my only simple brief is: whatever you do, make it easy for young people to access books and work to make books their best friends. Books for me are living life partners, and sharing a book is possibly the best way to make good friends too.

Innovation and Design

Is the education system helping us innovate or are we simply preparing the students to do assembly line work? The more uniform systems, curriculum and structure we put in place, the less our education system will deliver on innovation and design. When we give a block of wood with two basic tools like a mallet and a chisel to a young person, we make the person think, design and evolve. If we give Lego blocks, a kit to assemble an aero-model or simply use templates, we will stifle design and creativity. The kits and uniform building blocks are good business sense for marketers, less effort for teachers and easily help build prefab models which are misinterpreted as creation in our education system.

When children are given a container full of play dough or our good old plasticine, they make shapes and put thought to action. If we provide moulds/templates with the play dough, we make them use the shape and create a mere cast! Design is an evolution of vision and free thought, from chaos to order, from fuzzy logic to logic. The essence is freedom and the evolution of the mind. 'Jugaad', our frugal and flexible approach to innovation, has been the true spirit of an Indian. Innovation helps us do more with less, generates original ideas and pioneers growth. It all begins with an honest and true action guided by the free spirit of the young mind.

Frugality, flexibility and following our instincts are principles we all learned growing up in India. Intuition and immense adversity are at the root of the best ideas. In the West, innovation is done in Research and Development (R&D) departments; in India innovation happens at every corner of the street. As educators and trainers, it is our duty to provide an environment that helps a 'free mind' to design, and this is perhaps the only way to bring about innovation. The assembly line method of manufacturing built by Ford was indeed a way to mass produce with standards and today, we have China, the factory of the world.

Israel, the famous 'Start-Up Nation', has the maximum number of new enterprises listed on Wall Street. Silicon Valley, the mecca of innovation, finds that a large part of design and innovation originates from Israel. To 'process and build' is indeed good business but to 'design and innovate' has much greater value. If we do a 'me too' and look at our competition, we waste opportunity; if we reflect and think, we will create, and this is truly what education must help us to do. We do not always need a replica. There is a limit to what we can do with an assembly line. There is a lot for our educators to learn from the way the people of Japan and Israel look at innovation and design.

The charkha was believed to be a symbol of self-sufficiency during India's freedom movement, where each household was self-sufficient and innovated to build the nation. We will be happy when innovation is able to solve some of the daily problems faced by us. It is hard to believe that a caterpillar will transform one day, and a butterfly will fly free! Innovation and design alone can make the mind soar and conquer new frontiers.

In her piece titled 'What does "Made in India" Mean to the World' Kamini Banga says,

> Indian companies will find it very difficult to truly build a global brand till they invest in technology like Samsung and LG. Indian spend on R&D is about 0.9 per cent of GDP. This compares with China at 1.5 per cent of GDP which in absolute terms is second to the US! South Korea spends about 3.4 per cent of GDP, Japan about 3.5 per cent of GDP, and the US about 2.8 per cent of GDP. It almost appears that you need to spend about 3 per cent of GDP to be a world class leader in technological innovation.[23]

What does 'Made in India' stand for? This is a very difficult question and we need to ponder over this. Are we just the suppliers of low-end unskilled labour force or high-quality managers and talent to the world? If we want to lead the world and regain our lost glory, our education system and policy must encourage innovation and learning, not just focus on literacy statistics. Next time we go to a class full of innovative minds, we should make it our duty to help them think, design and innovate. Art and craft has been an intrinsic part of the Indian civilization, and yet we have not realized the true potential of innovation and design. The history of India shows our craftspeople were the leaders in design—the Taj Mahal, the famous forts and monuments that stand out in the

---

[23]Banga, K. (23 October 2012). *What does 'Made in India' mean to the world.* Economic Times Blog. Retrieved 16 June 2020, from https://economictimes.indiatimes.com/blogs/Globalpositioning/what-does-made-in-india-mean-to-the-world/

world were all designed by the creative Indian. Arayabhatta, Tagore, Raman, Chanakya, many leading minds and even a legend like Mahatma Gandhi were real innovators in their areas. Today we are becoming an assembly line of Japanese design, a producer of crops grown from imported seeds and sending out the best of Indian minds to empower nations all over the world.

A teacher alone can help build a great India by helping the young people lead in innovation and design. Let us not ape our competition, but be original as this alone will add the greatest value. Who knows the block of wood a teacher gives to the student will one day produce another marvel in design. The true Guru, teacher, today needs to be resurrected in our society and help the Shishya, student, reach his true potential. Innovation and design will only be possible when the teacher finds the rightful place in society and is able to be the true leader the society needs.

The time is now ripe for us to value our culture, develop an open learning environment and recommit ourselves to innovation and design. Gone are the days when we could pride ourselves with providing the world with engineers and doctors and do the low-end process delivery. We have to reclaim our true position as leaders and innovate to succeed.

The Art of Writing in School

In this world of electronic delivery, the art of writing could be the casualty. We live in an era of instant communication and are connecting with each other more. The need to be comprehensive in our writing is losing ground. SMS language, abbreviations and slang are corrupting the art of writing very rapidly. Business at the speed of thought sometimes even pushes us to share information without thought and editing. Writing has character, a physical form and conveys emotions far more efficiently. The written word is an art form in itself and is deeply personal too. With the proliferation of electronic and print media, who knows the handwritten word itself may become extinct shortly. With touch and voice pushing us to new frontiers with gadgets, we may even end up with a paperless world in some years ahead, and that would indeed be a heartbreak for the romantics, the writers and the creators of the cursive writing form.

> Beneath the rule of men entirely great
> The pen is mightier than the sword. Behold
> The arch-enchanter's wand!—itself is nothing!—
> But taking sorcery from the master-hand
> To paralyse the Cæsars, and to strike.
> The loud earth breathless!—Take away the sword—
> States can be saved without it!

The Art of Writing in School

The sentence (if not the idea, which had been expressed in various earlier forms) was coined by the English author Edward Bulwer-Lytton (1803–1873) in 1839 for his play *Richelieu; Or the Conspiracy*.[24]

The term 'handwriting' encompasses both printing and cursive styles and is separate from formal calligraphy or typeface. Because each person's writing is unique, it can be used to verify a document's writer, the deterioration of an individual's handwriting may also be a symptom or result of certain diseases.

Education at school starts with the learning of the alphabet and building up the art of writing. We all will remember how we first started our school with the single letters, and then the joining of letters to make words, the formation of sentences and finally moved on to the writing of statements and expressions.

The most creative experience for me was of our English class teacher making us write a 'Thought for the Week'. This was an even bigger challenge for me than to learn how to write. It made me think, have my imagination go wild, scribble and cross out, and finally have a simple and powerful handwritten piece ready for my Monday morning English class. Yes, we did not have the tools of word processing and perhaps spent a lot of time thinking and imagining, and this is why the quality of our writing was much better and perhaps more original too.

In my secondary school years, our House Master would push us to keep a journal and write a Daily Log. An excellent way to reflect, learn time management and, in a very subtle

---

[24]Lytton, E.B. *Richelieu: Or the Conspiracy.* (2016). Wentworth Press.

way, a way to help us improve our art of writing. Now, the ubiquitous Calendar Apps keep our logs and reminders!

While at school, we had to file reports of our school outings and mid-term excursions with sketches and photos incorporated. The essays and writings of people are curated in museums all over the world, and perhaps when we go back to the archives in our schools, we will be delighted to find some of our very own original writings. Trust me, this will be your most treasured moment!

In today's world, the art of writing is often a casualty of 'cut and paste'. When I sit down to write my blog every tenth day of the month, I find that more than concentrating on my writing I end up browsing. When we quote with reference it is research and not copying, and this is perhaps what takes us away from the original way of writing and doing deep research, thinking, scratching our heads and coming up with eloquent prose.

As the world becomes increasingly digital, writing becomes even more important. This is especially true for non-writers. If you work in an office, the majority of your communications are made of text by email or IM. Whether you like it or not, your ability to exchange ideas, collaborate with others and ultimately succeed hinges on the ability to write effectively.

K. Stone has laid out a process to help us write faster, better and easier. To follow up, here are 10 timeless tips[25] to help you improve style and substance, straight from the pens of humanity's finest authors.

---

[25]Stone, K. Pick the Brain | Motivation and Self Improvement. Retrieved 30 June 2020, from https://www.pickthebrain.com/

1. Cut the boring parts
2. Eliminate unnecessary words
3. Write with passion
4. Paint a picture
5. Keep it simple
6. Do it with love
7. Learn to thrive on criticism
8. Write all the time
9. Write what you know or what you want to know
10. Be unique and unpredictable

Any change in the world must be brought about by the power of expression, and writing is indeed the most powerful form of expression. It is original, thought-provoking and when used effectively will be the change in itself. How do we do this? Here you will find some examples of how the art of writing can be encouraged at an institutional level.

How to Encourage the Art of Writing?

Beyond the simple need to write an essay or do homework, the school may want to set up a Literary Club or a Literary Society. This will bring together young people with a shared passion. With peers in action, writing will definitely become very exciting. Have a writers' workshop at school, send out entries for essay and writing competitions at the inter-school or national level. Use the internet to set up blogs and have students participate in online events and literary chats. Even simpler, start publishing a School Weekly or share information in groups. I am happy to share as an example The School Weekly of The Fabindia School hosted on the blog www.bateduction.

com. It took the community nearly 100 weeks to finally start enjoying working for the weekly. Today the students look forward to Mondays, the day of The School Weekly.

In this media-barraged world, writing skills, turn of phrase and succinctly put together information are of great importance. At The Doon School, the art of writing plays a catalytic part in learning. *The Doon School Weekly (DSW)*, written and edited by the boys, has been in existence since 1936 and is much awaited at Saturday morning breakfast. *Prayas* and *Arpan* (Hindi) and *The Echo* (a biannual science publication) are also written, edited and published by the boys. The Yearbook, the School List and *The Doon School Information Review* are other key publications.

A simple school newsletter can be made by using any average word processing software today. Microsoft Word has templates for school newsletters and so do other websites; even GoogleDocs is a good tool for self-publishing. There are indeed many tools and software programs available for free—all you need to do is search!

Music and films today are not distributed with the same method and medium as in the last century. Books too are changing form and all this is perhaps a pointer that writing as a form may not be so personal anymore. However, the art of writing will always exist as it is the most powerful medium of communication for us. The medium of distribution may change, but the power of the written word in any form will never be diluted.

The Annual Day at School

*Focus on the child's strengths. Emphasise and
celebrate the child's 'island of competence'.*
—Pat Kozyra[26]

The best way to have young people perform is to celebrate every achievement and encourage every step they take. From a toddler's first step to a running child, there is a great deal of effort going into every moment, every development. Likewise, all students in every school do put in a great deal of effort in the calendar year, and what better than the Annual Day to celebrate their effort. The Annual Day helps us showcase our ability to connect, to collaborate, to communicate and to create. This is really the essence of good education delivery at school.

This day is not merely one to give away the annual prizes for achievement; it is also a day to gladden the hearts of the children, the teachers, the parents and the community. All stakeholders must be involved and get an opportunity to cherish the moment. Yes, with hundreds and sometimes even thousands connected with one school, it is a big challenge to

---

[26]The author would like to thank Pat Kozyra for the thoughts and inspiration to write.

give due regard and recognition to many deserving students. To overcome this challenge, we may consider organizing several occasions to help young people participate and find themselves. The only way to build leadership is to help an individual find their suitable area of excellence.

Personal and social development of a young person is possible with due emphasis on service, skill, sport and study. Some schools even have separate days to celebrate the four key areas of delivery. Yes, there are the Annual Sports Day and the Annual Prize Day (devoted to academics). We must celebrate the achievement of every individual, and in doing so it is most important never to compare one child with another. The schools must provide the opportunity to showcase diversity and engage as many students as possible in a wide array of opportunities. A musical concert or the sports day, wherein a large number of students participate and are all rewarded not because each will win a medal, but simply because each child will feel special to be a cynosure of some eyes and a favourite among their friends and parents too.

Experts in the field of education and child development tell us that building self-esteem is the key to successful living. Self-esteem is both a prerequisite and a consequence of academic success, and a dynamic relationship exists between self-esteem and skill development. Self-esteem is how we value ourselves, how we see ourselves, and how we feel about our achievements. (Winners believe in themselves!) Children don't invent a low self-image for themselves. They learn it from adults, mostly parents. Parents and teachers of children must note that having a good self-esteem is also the ticket for making good choices about their mind and body. If young people think they are important and appreciated, they will also become leaders of their group or community. The Annual Day and such events will show that sincere interest can be more effective and meaningful than praise.

Events at school like debating competitions, sports matches, skill exhibitions and excursions must have parents as invitees and even encourage them to participate. In many schools, the alumni and the parents get an opportunity to participate and get involved with the school community. All stakeholders must be part of the celebrations, in particular the annual day celebrations or even the prize giving. The events must have a youth icon or an impressive personality to speak to the students as they are always in search of role models in life. While selecting a chief guest or role model, we must find people who have excelled in service, skill, study and sport.

We need to remember that a child's self-esteem is determined by the conditional acceptance they receive from others and the unconditional acceptance they receive from the parents and their teachers. The child's self-esteem is determined by success in four areas:

- Social (acceptance and friendships)—grows by participation in events and activities.
- Competence (in a skill area)—gives new areas to excel to each individual.
- Physical (clothing, appearance)—needs to be appreciated.
- Character (effort, generosity)—is celebrated by participating in service, sport and activities.

It is extremely important to compliment people, to magnify their strengths and not their weaknesses.

Robert D. Ramsey, in *501 Ways to Boost Your Child's Self-Esteem*, talks about the various ways we can contribute to building a child's self-esteem. Some examples based on his book are given below[27]:

- Post the child's drawings and schoolwork in prominent places. That's what the soft boards, charts and other spaces in the school/home are for!
- Help the child to remember the good times and the good things they do. This celebration will be the essence of the personal and social development of the individual student.
- Don't stop giving the child accolades and cheers because you think they are grown up, getting old for display of affection is indeed a fallacy. We are never too old for a pat on the back in front of an audience!
- Always share with your child what the teachers have said about them. Silence in mentioning and celebrating the child's achievement is not good.
- End each year in the school by reviewing the past 12 months and the accomplishments of the child.

The Annual Day is a time to showcase creativity. Creativity lies at the heart of what it means to be human. Creativity is not just about the arts or certain people. We all have the capacity for creative thinking—for generating and extending ideas, suggesting hypotheses, applying imagination and looking for alternative innovative outcomes.

---

[27]Ramsey, R. D. *501 Ways to Boost Your Child's Self-Esteem*. (2002). McGraw Hill Professional.

Creativity seems to be a capacity that is separate from intelligence, and the ways these combine can lead to very different learning styles and levels of achievement. Children who score high on intelligence tests may not necessarily be creative. We need to celebrate the creativity in every child and make this our daily practice, find special days and events and ensure that we help every child share their passion.

The annual day celebrations of any school bring out the essence of the country's cultural diversity and rich heritage. This is why we must celebrate the annual day and more at the school.

Value each child as an individual with unique strengths, needs, interests and skills.

Schools Must Provide Knowledge, Not Mere Information

Learning at school must light the 'lamp of knowledge' in each one of us.

Knowledge is a familiarity, awareness or understanding of someone or something, such as facts, information, descriptions or skills, which are acquired through experience or education by perceiving, discovering or learning. Knowledge can refer to a theoretical or practical understanding of a subject. It can be implicit (as with practical skill or expertise) or explicit (as with the theoretical understanding of a subject); it can be formal or systematic. In philosophy, the study of knowledge is called epistemology. The philosopher Plato famously defined knowledge as 'justified true belief', though 'well-justified true belief' is more complete.

According to American philosopher Stanley Cavell, 'Knowledge acquisition involves complex cognitive processes: perception, communication and reasoning; while knowledge is also said to be related to the capacity of acknowledgment in human beings.'[28]

In the words of author Israelmore Ayivor, 'We are no

---

[28]Cavell, S. 'Knowing and Acknowledging'. In *Must We Mean What We Say?: A book of essays* (pp. 238-266). (2002). Cambridge University Press.

longer in the dispensation of age and experience. We are in the era of knowledge and information. Information leads a true leader and a true leader leads others.'[29] Our education process, however, leans more towards imparting information. It encourages rote learning, a memorization technique based on repetition. The idea is that one will be able to quickly recall the meaning of the material the more one repeats it. Alternatives to rote learning include meaningful learning, associative learning and active learning. This is where we must value the power of knowledge and work towards the development of the knowledge base and empowering our young people with thinking ability and acquisition of skills for life.

In *The Golden Notebook*, Doris Lessing writes,

> Ideally, what should be said to every child, repeatedly, throughout his or her school life is something like this: 'You are in the process of being indoctrinated. We have not yet evolved a system of education that is not a system of indoctrination. We are sorry, but it is the best we can do. What you are being taught here is an amalgam of current prejudice and the choices of this particular culture. The slightest look at history will show how impermanent these must be. You are being taught by people who have been able to accommodate themselves to a regime of thought laid down by their predecessors. It

---

[29] *25 top leadership and self leadership quotes by Israelmore Ayivor*. (27 August 2013). Life's Coach. Retrieved 22 June 2020, from https://israeliveonline.wordpress.com/2013/08/27/25-top-leadership-and-self-leadership-quotes-by-israelmore-ayivor/comment-page-1/

is a self-perpetuating system. Those of you who are more robust and individual than others will be encouraged to leave and find ways of educating yourself—educating your own judgements. Those that stay must remember, always, and all the time, that they are being moulded and patterned to fit into the narrow and particular needs of this particular society.[30]

Knowledge must help an individual grow their vision and thinking.

THE KNOWLEDGE PYRAMID

By volume — By value

Decreasing value ↓

- Vision and Strategy
- Unique IP
- Wisdom
- Expert Opinion
- Intelligence
- Information
- Data
- Hearsay, Rumour, Scuttlebutt

Increasing value ↑

On the left, we find that 'Information' is towards the bottom of the pyramid. Data (information) today is available in large

---

[30] *A quote from the golden notebook.* Goodreads, Meet your next favorite book. Retrieved 26 July 2020, from https://www.goodreads.com/quotes/5606-ideally-what-should-be-said-to-every-child-repeatedly-throughout

volume and the ability to comprehend big data to help us grow our intellect is what we need to develop. While information may be easy to find and assimilate, the learning process at school must help us to be analytical and empower us to find the leadership within.

Knowledge must help us put together a strategy and this will be the best value for our education curriculum to deliver. Schools must change to help us be empowered with the ability to think and move away from being mere processors of data. The CPU of a computer processes data to deliver us the precise bits and bytes we need, and this is precisely how our brains must also function. The lamp of knowledge must help throw light that travels a long distance, to show us the way ahead in life. There is a need to find the sharpest of rays to reach the level of learning that grows the inner self. The sharpest of the light rays will always travel the longest distance and this is the way to look at the rays of knowledge too. The experimental method used to teach must involve manipulating one variable to determine if changes in one variable cause changes in another variable. This method relies on controlled methods, random assignment and the manipulation of variables to test a hypothesis. The child must demonstrate the ability to assimilate and deliver, and not merely rote and roll out.

Barbara Schieffelin Powell is an international educational consultant in curriculum development, teacher education and evaluation. She has helped deliver The Fabindia School Leadership Development Project and has been instrumental in helping to deliver the mission and vision of the school. The Fabindia School has undergone a leadership change, encountered the resistance to efforts to improve teaching performance and begun the process of moving away from rote learning to more active learning. Early efforts at improving teacher performance, such as goal setting and classroom observation, were first vigorously resisted. The principal began with a careful programme of classroom observation and discussion with teachers. Teachers were exposed to examples of more active learning by visiting other schools.

The Fabindia School helped teachers and students to:

- Identify and build on their strengths
- Discover their leadership potential
- Become self-directed and collaborative learners
- Become contributing members of their communities

Even though the teachers themselves helped develop this vision, they have not yet adopted attitudes and practices that embody the said vision. The monthly teacher training workshops are structured to help teachers identify their strengths and become self-directed and collaborative learners. Creating a different school culture which engages teachers in a vibrant and ambitious learning community is an essential and painstaking process which only evolves over time.

As Powell states, 'We still have a long way to travel, but we're on the road.' After two years it should be clear (if there was any doubt) that building a professional culture in a school consists not of a quick fix solution but a complex effort to change the culture within which teachers work. It is often slow and hard work, but we have made progress and look forward to the next stage. Generating widespread organizational change requires a comprehensive approach.

Collaborative learning is a situation in which two or

more people learn or attempt to learn something together. Knowledge can only be built by collaborative learning and not by rote. Information delivery is a process, while knowledge assimilation is true learning. In the *Bhagavad Gita*, Krishna uses the term 'Lamp of Knowledge', and true knowledge is that which destroys the darkness of ignorance. We may start the journey of learning with information but must work to light the lamp of knowledge.

What do you think students are learning at school—not in terms of academic content, but in terms of life lessons and soft skills? Are they learning, for example, how to follow directions? How to interpret text? How to cooperate and collaborate? How to be open to new ideas? How to think critically? What skills do you think they will most need to succeed in career and life? It's time we think about these as we reshape our education systems and strategies.

Value of Liberal Arts Education

Rabindranath Tagore envisioned an education that was deeply rooted in one's immediate surroundings while also connected to the cultures of the wider world, predicated upon pleasurable learning and individualized to the personality of the child. He felt that a curriculum should revolve organically around nature, with classes held in the open air under the trees to provide for a spontaneous appreciation of the fluidity of the plant and animal kingdoms and seasonal changes.

Education is freedom with responsibility, and this is only possible when our minds are free. We learn to delve deep within and think how each of our actions will affect the people around us. My favourite poem is that of Tagore[31], and this is what the whole liberal arts philosophy is all about.

> Where the mind is without fear and the head is held high;
> Where knowledge is free;
> Where the world has not been broken up into fragments by narrow domestic walls;
> Where words come out from the depth of truth;
> Where tireless striving stretches its arms towards perfection;

---

[31] Tagore, R. *Gitanjali by Rabindranath Tagore.* Poetry Foundation. https://www.poetryfoundation.org/poems/45668/gitanjali-35

Where the clear stream of reason has not lost its way
into the dreary desert sand of dead habit;
Where the mind is led forward by thee into ever-widening thought and action—
Into that heaven of freedom, my Father, let my country awake.

The world today feels the need for liberal arts education much more than professional, vocational or technical curricula. The East scores over the West as historically, the former has been the cradle of civilizations and culture; the West today looks to the East for traditions and learning from the spiritual past. Education must not be experimental learning alone and should work to build our spiritual quotient. Education must help build our perception beyond the five senses: vision, hearing, smell, taste and touch. There are more than 14 different types of senses as suggested by psychologists; for example, there are many people who can sense impending weather changes. My mother could always sense when I was about to make a mess (the sense also known as 'eyes in the back of the head'). And many people feel that they can sense when someone else is looking at them. The study of liberal arts makes us go beyond the physical self and this is what makes it more interesting and relevant today.

The term 'education' encompasses a whole gamut of experiential learning which, in a school, is given through teachers in the classroom and often, more importantly, outside. It is the nature of the experience and how it is designed to be imparted that makes the difference between a good school and an ordinary school. A liberal arts education is beyond simple Q&A and is more like fuzzy logic; it helps us develop the creative infinite mind. The study of Science and Maths helps us become analytical and find simple solutions for everyday needs, while liberal arts helps us develop and go beyond the finite. Maths, Algebra, Geometry all work in the realm of cause and effect and limit us to finite answers. True freedom will only come about with the development of liberal arts education.

Many of the modern-day curriculums lay emphasis on developing an analytical mind. This is done with research and experiential learning. When I remember my school days, perhaps the most profound of learning experiences were the adventurous journeys and excursions. The mid-term break in many institutions is meant for the students to travel, explore and see the world. This is where beyond developing a great understanding of living together, we are given a feel of nature, and that the world outside the simple brick-and-mortar classroom offers immense learning. Knowledge put to practice brings about real learning. Most of the outward-bound experiences, the service projects and even the sports camps gave us an opportunity to develop as better human beings.

Artisanship and entrepreneur skills are passed over generations, and when I see the qualification levels of many such people, they are far more successful than those with professional, vocational or technical qualifications. These individuals have learnt the ways of the world and have a deeper understanding of nature as well as the resources they use for their livelihoods. The expertise of traditional medicine, home remedies and life skills that liberal education provides is far more complex than the learning of a classroom based on Science, Technology or Maths.

The leading universities in the USA and even the UK owe their eminence to liberal arts education. In his book *On the Purpose of a Liberal Education*, Robert Harris talks about how liberal education presents students with at least six major benefits[32]:

1. Liberal education teaches students how to think.
2. Liberal education teaches students how to learn.
3. Liberal education allows students to see things whole.
4. Liberal education enhances students' wisdom and faith.
5. Liberal education makes students better teachers.
6. Liberal education contributes to students' happiness.

Knowing more about life increases pleasure. Harris states, 'A cultivated mind enjoys itself and life,' and, 'knowledge makes you smarter and smarter makes you happier.' It has been proven that people who are highly educated have higher satisfaction in life. At the end of the day, we should all know what we are doing, which is one of the reasons to study liberally. We are all truly blessed to have the opportunity to be liberally educated, and I hope we take full advantage of its benefits as we learn, grow and develop.

---

[32]*Robert Harris's On the Purpose of a Liberal Arts Education*. Essays, Research Papers, Term Papers, Internet Public Library. Retrieved 10 July 2020, from https://www.ipl.org/essay/Robert-Harriss-On-The-Purpose-Of-A-FJSCZBRSQG

Good Schools Should Offer Quality Liberal Arts Education

As Thomas Henry Huxley puts it succinctly,

> That man, I think, has had a liberal education who has been so trained in youth that his body is the ready servant of his will, and does with ease and pleasure all the work that, as a mechanism, it is capable of; whose intellect is a clear, cold, logic engine, with all its parts of equal strength, and in smooth working order; ready, like a steam engine, to be turned to any kind of work, and spin the gossamers as well as forge the anchors of the mind; whose mind is stored with a knowledge of the great and fundamental truths of Nature and of the laws of her operations; one who, no stunted ascetic, is full of life and fire, but whose passions are trained to come to heel by a vigorous will, the servant of a tender conscience; who has learned to love all beauty, whether of Nature or of art, to hate all vileness, and to respect others as himself. (Science & Education, of Huxley's Collected Essays)[33]

While Science and Medicine help us with solutions, and technology gives us convenience, it is the empathy and understanding of human nature which alone helps us become better human beings. Today we find that the world is showing a renewed interest in the study of liberal arts and needs this as a 'saviour of humanity'. Good schools should offer quality liberal arts education.

---

[33]Huxley, T.H. *Collected Essays*. (2011). Cambridge University Press.

Humanity Must Learn Humanities

It may be by coincidence or true design, but the study of sciences in the modern world has been accompanied by the rise of crime and violence in the world. Are we to look at history and see how the human values and quality of life have changed with the advent of the age of modern science?

Students are made to choose between the science stream and humanities in the Indian education system and they do not really have the freedom to choose what they want to study, with whom they would like to study and how they want to learn. What we refer to as basic life skills and the needs of a society are not what science teaches. While science offers us tools to be analytical and offers a logical understanding of the material being, an understanding of humanities is indeed more crucial for us to build a social and just society today. Science may help us build our ability to reason, but it is the humanities that will make us think and reflect, and even more valuable are the soft skills that are the bedrock of human understanding. Study of humanities to me is about 'being human' and developing a feel for life. The word 'human' is very much a part of 'humanities'; the need of this stream in our scope of study is indeed paramount.

In the modern age, where economies are neither being run by the blue-collar and, strictly speaking, nor the white-collar workforce, it is even more important for us to see how important the humanities is for building a better world. Science has evolved, and so has man's ability to challenge nature. As we produce more with the help of science, we also create more waste, crime and destruction and are headed to become a very unhappy consumerist society. The need for values and soft skills that come to us through our study of the humanities is the need of the hour. In Delhi University, the top three women's colleges are also the best performing in the humanities stream. Liberal Arts and the study of subjects like English Literature alone help us build the qualities of empathy, compassion, understanding and some may say morals and values. What is needed is value-based education and not just a debate between humanities and science.

A country like Bhutan values itself as being high on the 'happiness index', the search for peace and happiness in the mystic Himalayas and the cures provided by traditional/natural medicine all strengthen the belief that science does not always lead to human development. We need a spiritual self that is evolved, and that places human feeling and well-being above the simple study of logic and a questioning mind.

Humans need to study humanity, and being human is our first duty! It may sound like a cliché and may make way for us to wonder whether we have taught science the right way. Subject boundaries like the physical and gender divide have been created by practitioners and schools that want to maximize profits in the delivery of education as an economic activity. The great minds, philosophers, spiritualists and geniuses did not choose between humanities or science. They were all humanists who used science as a tool to further their understanding of humans.

The need of the hour is to be more liberal and use the fuzzy logic approach and deal with reasoning that is approximate rather than fixed and exact. This will help us value the study of humanities to further learning and help the human mind evolve to an advanced level, and not just push us to become scientists or mathematicians alone.

The study of humanities will lead us to a more value-based and learned society. The education system needs to be delivered as an economic model, and learning should be the key objective and not a mere outcome. Science is easy to teach and deliver, while humanities is infinite and we do need to do a lot of research and reading to help build ourselves to be learned individuals. This is what perhaps makes the delivery of science and a world full of inventions produce goods, services and products that do not really help further humanity. The atomic bomb is the most extreme example of the use of science, which has led to create a world full of hatred and division. The learning of the mahatmas, spiritual gurus and preachers continue to act as balm and offer peace of mind to humanity.

New Teaching and Learning Approaches

Think how teaching has changed, is changing and will keep changing. New learning approaches and innovation in teaching made us venture out to explore the idea of collaborating with the teaching community and understand what it means to put in place a Change Creation System.

Many teaching approaches of earlier times predate much of the scientific knowledge about learning and intellectual development. The processes and day-to-day work limits the time in hand with the teachers. The information explosion and unlimited supply of data make learning a bigger challenge. Where do we start and how do we make learning more meaningful?

Teachers need to think, inquire, plan, modify and test new teaching and learning approaches. The quest for learning is a hunger, a passion and the more we share the more we learn. Learning theory (education) is a conceptual framework that describes how information is absorbed, processed and retained during learning. Cognitive, emotional and environmental influences, as well as prior experience, all play a part in how understanding, or a worldview, is acquired or changed, and knowledge and skills retained.

In *Schools Can Change*,[34] the authors state that the learning teacher cannot ignore research, including research analysis, behaviour analysis, collaborate in learning, reflect, stimulate learning strategies and must be subject to assessment and tested for use of technology.

The schools generally follow a cycle of work in their course of the year. This often leaves no scope to experiment and learn. We end up as a mere assembly line in manufacturing parlance. There is the inherent need for a five-step process to make a breakthrough and put in place a Change Creation System.

First, all the faculty and leaders in the school must identify the learning needs and form action teams. A good example is of a rural English-medium school where the leadership set itself a goal of making their school the 'best English-medium school in the area'. This need gave a direction for the action teams to move ahead and explore how this was to be made possible. Action teams were created for understanding the needs of the students and the teachers.

The second step involves the action team setting out to create an action plan. The areas of focus include training of faculty to deliver better, use of technology and mapping the needs of the students.

The third step is the implementation of the inquiry areas to change and practice and improve student learning. While the needs of the teachers and their challenges are the key focus, at no stage should the goal of helping learning and quality delivery in the classroom be compromised.

---

[34]Lick, D.W., Clauset, K.H., & Murphy, C.U. *Schools Can Change: A Step-by-step Change Creation System for Building Innovative Schools and Increasing Student Learning.* (2012). Corwin Press.

The fourth step involves the assessment of impact of the action teams' work on teacher practice and student learning.

The fifth step involves the sharing of results and best practices across the school, and applying lessons learned.

The right leadership understands the vision and kick-starts the change creation process. When we experiment with new teaching and learning approaches, the outcome will be improved student learning. The cycle will continue and the concentric circles of the process will help us build our unique teaching and learning approaches.

Teachers may change assumptions about their self-esteem and professionalism through systemic efforts. Like doctors and lawyers, our teachers are real professionals and we must encourage them to take more responsibility for actions. They are not a mere process or a system, but are the real changemakers.

Teaching and learning are simply two sides of the same coin, and can never work in isolation. The most important point is that in the learning environment our currency is young people, and this makes the delivery process most crucial. We have to test ourselves and ensure we do our homework, not just absolve ourselves from our position of learners first and put the onus on our pupils, who by force of circumstance have to resort to rote learning.

Rote Learning or Understanding?

Some students are skilled at rote learning for exams, whereas others perform better when they have understood the concept. Which of these do you consider a better approach? New teaching and learning approaches are always in a dilemma regarding the needs and the abilities of the students. We must never lose sight of the fact that in the world where we have an overload of information and access has become easy over the years, teachers will have to use innovative ways to help their pupils learn. If a teacher has to earn, they must first learn!

Disciplined leaders and teachers align with the school's vision and have a clear understanding of who they are and where they are going. For any consistent framework to deliver, it is imperative that the experiments in learning are not looked at as a simple cost, but as an opportunity cost to deliver new teaching and bring about a paradigm shift in the way we deliver learning in a classroom. New teaching and learning approaches are most crucial for innovation, and as mentioned earlier we often get too absorbed in the process of the school delivery cycle. In our quest of profit maximizing, we often do not invest enough in new ways of knowledge delivery. Please note that simply investing in technology is not the solution; in order for any learning to build up, there is the need for the action teams to reflect within and look at their future as professional learners and not mere teachers.

Teachers learn best when they work together to solve common problems. You may consider joining the Learning Forward network of teacher leaders at www.learningforward.org, and get resources, tools, strategies and access to committed colleagues willing to share their expertise and experience to develop solutions to the issues you're facing in your school and classroom. Schools can change, and this is only possible when new teaching and learning become the DNA of the organization.

Freedom to Perform

Performance as a parameter to deliver, as a qualitative or even a quantitative measure, makes learning a challenge. What is more pertinent is the 'freedom to perform'. As often stated, the aim of education is independence, and education will accomplish this aim only when there is full freedom to choose what one would like to do, how one would like to do it and with whom. The education system often, under the garb of delivery and process, limits our freedom to perform.

Some decades ago, I had wanted to study Biology with Geography, but this was not possible as such a choice did not fit into the bundled offerings of the school and the education board. I moved on and found that my marks or the quantitative measure of my ability would only let me do a graduation in Economics in the university of my choice. Here was a student who loved the outdoors and had a natural love for Geography, but he went on to become a business person post a degree in Law and a professional programme from IIM.

Often circumstances restrict our freedom to choose and thus limit our performance.

A genius is a person who displays exceptional intellectual ability, creativity or originality, typically to a degree that is associated with the achievement of unprecedented insight.

There is no scientifically precise definition of genius, and the question of whether the notion itself has any real meaning has long been a subject of debate. The term is used in various ways: to refer to a particular aspect of an individual, or the individual in his or her entirety; to a scholar in many subjects (e.g. Gottfried Wilhelm Leibniz or Leonardo da Vinci) or a scholar in a single subject (e.g. Albert Einstein or Charles Darwin). Research into what causes genius and mastery is still in its early stages, and psychology offers relevant insights.[35]

From chaos to creativity, from clutter to a 'eureka moment', all great people have followed their heart. They have been much appreciated despite the fact when doing their good work their freedom to perform may have been scoffed at. The landscape has since changed for the better. Today we do find parents, teachers and mentors doing their best to help young people excel with passion and choice. Parents now want their children to play sports, they do find the passion in the young people and are now looking up to them, appreciating them and some are even letting the youth follow their heart. The world today has become flat and travel has become a part of life; opportunities too have grown manifold. In times where innovation is now the key for leadership, the freedom to perform is indeed the most essential element to help each person develop as an individual and attain true glory.

In the education system some have a choice for what to study, but how to study is still governed by a curriculum. There is a choice of the board one can choose and today, the

---

[35]*IELTS Reading: Match the Names.* (21 July 2014). IELTS Simon. Retrieved 20 July 2020, from https://ielts-simon.com/ielts-help-and-english-pr/2014/07/ielts-reading-match-the-names.html

idea of Geography with Biology is indeed a reality. When we give due regard to informal education and not use the paper degree as a measure, will there be true freedom? There are limited experiments where one can choose what to study, how to study and with whom to study; however, is there a choice to not study?

What is studied will be a debate always and will be hemmed in the boundary of education systems, economics of delivery and so-called social practices. What is most important then is that Service, Skill, Sport and Study are all forms or rather integral parts of the education process and time has now come for us to offer the freedom to choose from these too.

Performance is a yardstick that will change; an individual must follow the heart and work passionately to find oneself. The sky is the limit and innovation is the key. Let us all rededicate ourselves to ensure that freedom to perform becomes a fundamental purpose of life.

SECTION III

LESSONS FOR LIFE

What Education Does

I believe there's a hero in us all that keeps us honest, gives us strength, makes us noble, and finally allows us to die with pride.

—Mike Saquan Wren[36]

Is going to school at the core of good education? Why do successful people walk tall? It all leads us to explore how we build self-confidence and make success a habit. An excellent institution—whether a family or even a school—should help us walk with pride and build our emotional quotient.

I feel education should empower us to walk with confidence. When we look at schools that work to deliver education, we find that not many will help us achieve the key purpose, as these institutions look at education as a commodity and sell it to us as a package. The main motive of most of these schools is to run a sustainable business; this often will not let them deliver value and meet our purpose of helping

---

[36]Wren, M.S. *I believe there's a hero in us all*. Search Quotes. Retrieved 10 June 2020, from https://www.searchquotes.com/quotation/I_believe_there%27s_a_hero_in_us_all_that_keeps_us_honest%2C_give_us_strength%2C_makes_us_noble%2C_and_final/434241/

us build confidence. The school may give us literacy, but this is not what education is all about.

Education has helped to make me who I am. Through education, I learned more about my strengths and weaknesses. It helped me develop both occupations and vocations. It gave me confidence and helped me to see the world as an approachable place.

Evaluating People vs Their Education

In 'What Does It Mean to Be Well-Educated'[37], Alfie Kohn asks:

> Does the phrase 'well-educated' refer to a quality of the schooling you received, or to something about you? Does it denote what you were taught, or what you learned (and remember)? If the term applies to what you now know and can do, you could be poorly educated despite having received a top-notch education. However, if the term refers to the quality of your schooling, then we'd have to conclude that a lot of 'well-educated' people sat through lessons that barely registered, or at least are hazy to the point of irrelevance a few years later.

According to the panellists of the Askwith Forum at Harvard, in order to be considered educated, students should leave school with a deep understanding of themselves and how they fit into the world and have learned what some call 'soft skills'—complex problem-solving, creativity, entrepreneurship,

---

[37] Kohn, A. (19 March 2017). *What does it mean to be well-educated?* Alfie Kohn. Retrieved 30 June 2020, from https://www.alfiekohn.org/article/mean-well-educated-article/

the ability to manage themselves and the ability to be lifelong learners. As Professor Fernando Reimers, who moderated the panel, summarized, there is a disconnect between how education gets delivered in the classroom and the common desire for students to become good, well-rounded people.

How do we empower young people to walk with confidence? This is the dilemma that will never be resolved, as we all have our very personal views and beliefs. The culture, stereotypes and the work of generations cloud our minds and often make us feel incomplete and demolish our confidence. How do we overcome negativity and build our self-confidence? Learning is an integral part of our life and education should not only stimulate us but free us and empower us to find ourselves. I have often said that 'leadership is finding yourself', and a leader is a person who can walk with confidence. Education should help us be the leader we want to be, and not cage our thoughts and make us hostage to a curriculum.

Dale Carnegie shows us how to develop poise, gain self-confidence, improve memory, make our meaning clear, begin and end a talk, interest and charm our audience, improve our diction and win an argument without making enemies. In his bestselling book *How to Develop Self-Confidence and Influence People by Public Speaking*, he offers hundreds of practical and valuable tips on influencing the important people in your life: your friends, your customers, your business associates and your employees. This book has been tested and used successfully by millions of people all over the world.[38]

---

[38] *How to Develop Self-confidence and Influence People*. Goodreads | Meet your next favorite book. Retrieved 30 June 2020, from https://www.goodreads.com/book/show/4868.How_to_Develop_Self_Confidence_And_Influence_

Our education process should help us walk tall; we should be able to understand our inner self, and express our heart with the effective use of our intelligence. Education will only be complete when we follow our heart, stand on our feet and walk with our heads held high. The mind thus must be empowered and not merely filled with information like bits and bytes in the CPU of a computer. Over the years, mind mapping has been extensively studied, and it has been found that verbalization often devalues the core of learning and that the written word seems to be the only way to grow literacy and this itself is the biggest challenge.

The economist Tyler Cowen speculates:

> Men are born beasts. But education gives you a peer group, a self-image, and some skills as well. Getting an education is like becoming a Marine. Men need to be made into Marines. By choosing many years of education, you are telling yourself that you stand on one side of the social divide. The education itself drums that truth into you.[39]

Our minds are by far the greatest mechanism we can ever possess, yet we hardly take notice of it. My friend and author Ted Falconar shared with me a vision: we are now engaged in promoting the Creative Infinity Mind that is the mystic and scientific wonderland, a Renaissance that humanity has

---

People

[39] *Why education is productive—a parable of men and beasts—Marginal revolution.* (2 February 2006). Marginal REVOLUTION. Retrieved 30 June 2020, from https://marginalrevolution.com/marginalrevolution/2006/02/why_education_i.html

hardly embarked upon being at an early stage in its evolution; the single dimensioned verbal mind, that is spiritual poverty lacking beauty, creativity and imagination is still hampering the world. Education as it stands today kills creativity and makes us our mere verbalizers, taking from us the opportunity to be great visualizers.

Intellectual ability refers to content and level of cognition ('What?' and 'How much?'). Cognitive style reflects manner or mode of cognition ('How?'). The term 'cognitive style' is associated with stable, trait-like consistency in personal approach to attending, perceiving and thinking. Or, cognitive styles are particular personality-determined modes of perceiving, remembering, thinking and problem-solving. Another definition: Cognitive styles represent stable traits that distinguish the learners according to consistencies in interacting with the environment. Cognitive styles might be understood better by comparing them to construct cognitive ability within a dichotomy-based conceptual framework.[40]

We will only walk with confidence when we begin to understand ourselves, and education is only one of the tools for us to find our own self. Education must free our mind and not enslave us to a system. We not only need IQ but most of all a great level of EQ (Emotional Quotient). We will only walk with confidence when we are emotionally strong, and this is what we need at the core of any learning delivered by any institution. We will need the strength of spiritual insight to support our ardour.

---

[40]Cognition. Department of Information Technologies. Retrieved 30 June 2020, from https://www-it.fmi.uni-sofia.bg/courses/Demand/module3/unit5/sub1.htm

School Bell: The First Lesson in Management

You will definitely hear the school bell ring in your head, whenever you lend your ear to it! The sound of the school bell has a certain amount of energy that makes the adrenaline flow and makes us look forward to the next hour.

The first bell of the day brings in great energy, as enthusiastic young and fresh minds race to the school gates. The day will see the entry and exit of fun and joy in the class, till the last bell that leaves the campus devoid of all energy, making it seem like sunset hour at midday.

Our first lessons in time management perhaps are rendered to us by this innocuous bell that may sound jarring at first but becomes part of our growing up years. A school period is a block of time allocated for lessons, classes or other activities in schools. They typically last between 40 and 60 minutes, with around three to eight periods per school day. Educators determine the number and length of these periods and may even regulate how each period will be used.

Managing time is really the first challenge for all of us at school. Capturing the imagination and making sure that the 40 odd minutes lead to learning is always the biggest challenge for teachers and students alike.

School Bell: The First Lesson in Management 109

Our first lessons in time management perhaps are rendered to us by this innocuous bell. The race against time, the need to complete the lesson plan, ensure good understanding and give the students the real joy of learning between two bells is not an easy task for even the best of teachers. How best you use your limited time determines your effectiveness as a teacher or a mentor for a group of learners. There are thus crucial questions to be answered keeping in mind that the next bell will ring soon: What do I do? When do I do it? How well do I do it?

Is time management an issue for your students? Do their busy schedules and social lives prevent them from completing homework assignments? Managing time is the most important element as it is the basic premise of our putting in place a timetable; the bells for the hour are the key to effective delivery. The timetable adds up to the calendar and this makes the academic year for our curriculum delivery.

It is often said that students who have studied in residential schools are more independent and parents may be of the opinion that they have greater confidence. This is merely because the school works hard to make best use of the full 24 hours they have at hand. From the wake-up bell to the lights out bell all members of the school community put in work to synchronize the life of a child at school. As the average boarding school child hears more bells, I am taking the risk of stating that perhaps these children become more capable at managing their time. When the children return home from boarding school, initially they find the going tough, but then they feel the urge to do something and put forth the question, 'What do I do?'

A bell is a signal in a school that tells the students when

it is time to go to class in the morning and when it is time to change classes during the day. Typically, the first bell tells the students that it is time to report to class and the bell that occurs shortly after that means that the students are late. There may also be a warning bell between the first bell and the late bell.

The signal for us to thus get active is really the school bell. The ringing sound may excite us or push us. It definitely is the call of the hour and wants us to know that precious time is ticking. Successful people know how to manage their time better, and leadership in my opinion is really best of time management. If you learn how to use your time most judiciously, you will succeed. This is what we will have a parent telling a child at home and the school bell reminding us at school. It is important for you to hear the bell ring and value your most precious moments in time.

How to Manage Your Time

Time seems to be at a premium these days. We have devices that keep us constantly connected with work, with friends and family and more. This may seem to create some form of stress and challenge you to keep up the pace. All you need to do is put in place your 'things to do' at the early hour or at the first bell, and then do your best to follow it through the day. We must never panic or be stressed, but must appreciate that a moment in time is perhaps the most precious and, like flowing water, it will never come back.

Our life indeed sets a limit of time, and this is indeed the wealth we often do not value in our quest for materials and the race to beat the others to it.

Hear the bell, find the energy, think for yourself and make a conscious decision as to how best you will use your time. Remember the school bell and hear it ring always. Let it not make life uncomfortable but instead help you enjoy every moment and be the master of your time. Time management alone will help you find yourself and live a joyous life.

Going to School

Do we ever graduate from the school of learning?
Many may say that their school life comes to an end when they graduate from a school to move up the employment ladder. This, in fact, is just the beginning, as when you are in knowledge acquisition mode you are the receiver and this is what schools today deliver. When we move on to learning for life, get real and value the application of knowledge at work or in life, our wealth of knowledge starts growing dramatically. While K-12 is often thought of as the schooling process, in reality, it is just the infancy. Yes, some gifted and genius young minds are way ahead of the rest, yet the learners work their way up and as we grow in life all move to the infinite zone.

Knowledge is infinite. It is not defined by a score and so how can we ever leave school! The school is where learning is embedded and life itself is the biggest learning. Acquisition of knowledge is really the development of a fertile mind, and as our mind crosses the frontiers of learning we move on in life. Words and language are the tools of knowledge building, it is only when we have our extra sensory perception evolve do we actually start getting the dividend of going to school. Yes, learning is the biggest giver of joy and freedom to an individual and the key to quality in education. As we grow, we find that the best part of school was the fun and the carefree nature of life. For us to grow our minds we must appreciate the joy of learning and not just consider going to school as a basic necessity of our modern society.

Learning is a gift and the more we value this, the more will we appreciate the meaning of life. Life begins with learning, flowers with learning and learning never stops at any point in our lives. When we look at the philosophy of the creative infinity mind, we see that the school of learning empowers us by taking us on a journey to find ourselves. Successful are the people who are able to delve within, reflect, learn and lead their own lives. Education is freedom with responsibility, and learning is the bedrock of education.

Yes, we build schools; but that isn't enough. To create lasting change, we must never graduate from the learning environment and this is what we all must appreciate about the schooling process. A school is an environment and not a structure. It is an ecosystem and it will indeed be apt to say that life is the school for the living!

Learning: From Isolation to Collaboration

Learning happens when we begin our journey in the world as individuals and learn to collaborate. No learning will ever occur in isolation. It is a collaborative exercise that perhaps helps you become a thinking person. Knowledge is a product while learning is the relentless pursuit of developing one's abilities and an effort to understand the ways of the world.

Learning is a process and not an event. Individuals accomplish it, and it is indeed a highly personal experience. It involves developmental growth and is best understood as the change we go through in our journey of life. The most important point to note is that 'learning is greater than change'. For learning to thrive, we need to adapt; our mindset and behaviour need to change.

In isolation we are cocooned from the need to move beyond our comfort zone; we need to break out and learn to challenge ourselves to deliver as a team player. The community is indeed a reflection of individuals that make up the society. It is how we collaborate that brings about transformational change and helps us grow as individuals and as a community too. A school of ants can work to move the largest obstacle, but in isolation a single ant may not have the wherewithal to make a difference.

Ant societies have a division of labour, communication between individuals and the ability to solve complex problems. These parallels with human societies have long been an inspiration and subject of study. Humans are social beings and need to connect, communicate and collaborate to create. Learning will only happen when we work together. The human form is itself brought about when the isolated sperm meets the egg, thus further confirming the fact that 'isolation' is not the DNA of any life form.

Yes, scientists and even gurus in their quest may want a peaceful abode. Their work will only reach the collaborators when they spread the word to help learn. A teacher in a class is a learner first and then a mentor, and no teacher can work in isolation. Learning, being a social exercise, helps us make a better world and share the best practices.

In *Love—The Key to Optimism: Path towards happiness*,[41] Roshan D. Bhondekar says,

> Learning is the act of acquiring new, or modifying and reinforcing, existing knowledge, behaviours, skills, values, or preferences and may involve synthesizing different types of information. The ability to learn is possessed by humans, animals, and some machines. Progress over time tends to follow learning curves. Learning is not compulsory; it is contextual. It does not happen all at once, but builds upon and is shaped by what we already know. To that end, learning may be viewed as a process, rather than a collection of factual and procedural knowledge.

---

[41]Bhondekar, R.D. *Love—The Key to Optimism: Path towards Happiness.* (2015). Notion Press.

In Sociology, we define isolation as the 'social lack of contact between persons, groups or whole societies. In Psychology, it is 'the failure of an individual to maintain contact with others or genuine communication where interaction with others persists'. Both the definitions make it very clear that if there is no cross-fertilization of thought and human connectivity, there will be no learning.

Learning may occur as a result of habituation or classical conditioning, seen in many animal species, or as a result of more complex activities such as play, seen only in relatively intelligent animals. Learning may occur consciously or without conscious awareness.

Learning is the transition from isolation to collaboration. The classroom is the ecosystem for learning and here the students and the teacher collaborate to further their abilities and grow their knowledge base. The application of knowledge is the real meaning of education, and we all must work for bringing the necessary change in our lives.

Teachers Travel with You All Your Life

Learning is a lifelong process and so it is vital that we have the best teacher accompany us on the journey of life. We may grow up and follow a guru or a mentor. Whomsoever we follow, the teacher's leadership is supreme; the teacher travels with us for life. The empathy and care our teachers bestow on us will be etched in our memory for life. No matter where we go, we will always carry our teacher in us.

What Makes a Teacher Great?

There are characteristics that can predict whether a teacher will be a great teacher even before they get into the classroom. Studies show that the teacher is one of the most crucial factors in a child's school success. A poor teacher can set a child back forever while a great one will inspire them forever.

I discovered some great poetry in Kozyra's book *Tips and Tidbits for Parents and Teachers*:

> I am a counsellor and psychologist to a problem-filled child,
> I am a police officer that controls a child one wild.
> I am a travel agent scheduling our trips for the year,
> I am a confidante that wipes a crying child's tear.

I am a banker collecting money for a ton of different things,
I am a librarian showing adventures that a storybook brings.
I am a custodian that has to clean certain little messes,
I am a psychic that learns to know all that everybody only guesses.
I am a photographer keeping pictures of a child's yearly growth,
When mother and father are gone for the day, I become both.
I am a doctor that detects when a child is feeling sick,
I am a politician that must know the laws and recognise a trick.
I am a party planner for holidays to celebrate with all,
I am a decorator of a room, filling every wall.
I am a news reporter updating on our nation's current events,
I am a detective solving small mysteries and ending all suspense.
I am a clown and comedian that makes the children laugh,
I am a direction ensuring they have lunch or from mine I give them half.
When we seem to stray from values, I become a preacher,
I'm proud to say, "I am a teacher."

Children require guidance and sympathy and not mere instructions. The degree and certificates a teacher carries will not be of any use, if there is no empathy and concern for the child in the teacher. You do not need a classroom to teach;

what you need is a heart with all the room. Look back and recollect the best teacher who touched your heart, who made you feel very special and who had full faith in your ability. A teacher is with you all your life. Even today I remember my first teacher in Kindergarten, my special teacher in Class I and others who have helped me find myself. Their love and care irrespective of domain knowledge will always carry me for life.

As we grow up, we strike a chord with a guru or a mentor and sometimes the person is even a colleague. Learning is from the heart; the mind is a mere knowledge bank. For effective learning the teacher must become an integral part of our life. It is the true disciple who becomes most successful and inherits the mantle of the successful leader.

Writer and educational consultant Mark F. Goldberg states: 'Greatness in teaching is just as rare as greatness in medicine, dance, law, or any other profession. Although the qualities that make great teachers are not easy to inculcate or duplicate, understanding these qualities can give all teachers a standard of excellence to strive for, and guide schools in their efforts to recruit and retain the best teachers.'[42]

You may not always find the real teacher in the classroom, as the walls often box the learning process. The teacher has the burden of the curriculum, the challenge of living up to expectations, the need to work for a livelihood and finally Key Result Areas (KRA) to meet! A teacher is one who will be part of your life's journey, who you will love, adore and even try to emulate. For me the classroom is a mere brick-and-mortar

---

[42]Goldberg, M. F. 'The qualities of great teachers.' In *M. Scherer (Ed.), Keeping good teachers.* (2003). ASCD.

location and not a place of real life learning. When you start limiting the learning to hours, books and time, you will have a challenge at hand.

In our journey we have had the opportunity to travel with many co-travellers. As Dr Mary Kay Whitaker, a business leadership strategist, executive coach, trainer, author and founder of the About Leaders community and drMaryKay.com, says,

> Think back to a great teacher you've had in your life. Maybe there was an exceptional teacher who encouraged you and helped you explore future career opportunities that would incorporate your talents. Maybe you had a coach who not only taught you how to do a perfect lay-up, but also reminded you about the importance of getting good grades in addition to high scores. How about your friends or parents and all the lessons they may have taught you: to push yourself to succeed, to do the things you love, to believe that you can be or do anything that you set your mind to.[43]

The teachers who have been a part of my life taught me how to appreciate others, care for nature and play the game to find the joy within. When climbing mountains, doing a cross country run, cooking at home, standing up and speaking... all they said was follow your heart, be true to yourself and you will find the leader within. Being a person with no particular religious beliefs, I am sure when you hold someone in high

---

[43] *A great leader = a great teacher.* (7 May 2019). AboutLeaders. Retrieved 15 July 2020, from https://aboutleaders.com/leadership-skills-9-a-great-leader-a-great-teacher/#gs.99tl9g

esteem you will carry that person in your heart—and it is this person who I would call your teacher. Some may say you are a follower, but remember you are simply travelling with your teacher and doing it at your own comfort and pace too.

Teachers have faith in you; this is why you never get lost! In my school days, a group of us boys went trekking. There were no mobile phones in those days and we lost our way. After a day's delay, when our parents and the community would have gone wild, my teacher was very comforting and simply assured all of them that we will find our way. The great teacher had an intuition and tremendous faith in the ability of his pupils. When we finally trooped in a day late, he was ready to welcome us with a plum cake and very eager to hear our experience and exploits. There he was, smiling warmly and with a heart full of compassion and care, standing by the boys for their efforts. Note there was no panic, no chastizing, no questioning, just celebrating the spirit of exploration and faith in the 'shishya' (student).

Stories and fond memories are treasures we all share. This is where the teacher must be the most prolific artist. Your favourite teacher will be able to correlate reel life with real life and make every moment a moment of learning. It is very important for us to understand that learning has to precede teaching. While teaching may be a process, the outcome has to be learning and that too learning for life. Find the teacher you cherish and travel with the individual for life. Let your teacher reside in your heart, and you will be able to overcome any major challenge or obstacle in the journey of life.

As Swami Vivekananda said, 'You have to grow from the inside out. None can teach you, none can make you spiritual.

There is no other teacher but your own soul.'

Caring in abundance, having the desire to find out more, cherishing the students, knowing them very well and being a knowledgeable person will to deliver enable you lifelong learning. This is the teacher you will travel with all your life.

Personal and Social Development at School

The best way to deliver quality education and bring about the personal and social development of an individual is by empowering young people to follow their passion.

The education process today is built on the 4S approach: Service, Skill, Sport and Study. The CBSE, CISCE and most of the national boards are now adding skills and activities beyond the classroom to their curriculum. Each of these four dimensions of learning are equally essential to help young people find themselves and be the leaders they aspire to be.

A good school must work to help provide the best ecosystem for the personal and social development of an individual. This will only happen when we focus beyond studies. We need to lay equal emphasis on Service, Skill, Sport and Study.

Service, Community Service or Social Service has been an integral part of The Doon School since its inception. The first headmaster, Mr Arthur Foot believed that 'the boys should leave The Doon School as members of an aristocracy, but it must be an aristocracy of service inspired by ideas of unselfishness, not one of privilege, wealth or position.' For decades since then, this has been one of the foundation principles of the school. Over the years The Doon School has accumulated an enviable record of service. The school boys have always lent their helping hand, across India, to people affected by the worst hit earthquakes, tsunamis, landslides and floods. For instance, during the 1991 Uttarkashi earthquake, when all communication lines were down, the school's HAM radio club joined hands with the state administration and aid-providers to set up channels of communication with the base station. When the COVID19 pandemic struck the country in 2020, the members of The Doon School Old Boys' Society just rolled up their sleeves and formed teams to help not only people in distress but also supported the health workers and civil services with resources and volunteered often at their own peril.

All boys of The Doon School have to complete mandatory hours of social service. The school runs a *Panchayat Ghar* where the students teach the underprivileged children. The School has, over the years, adopted villages and worked with the villagers in the construction of houses, community centres and school buildings, sanitation systems, energy efficiency systems, self-employment and small-scale irrigation systems. Apart from village development, the school is actively involved with the Raphael Ryder Cheshire International Centre and the Cheshire Home.

Skill aims to encourage the development of personal interests and practical skills. Music, Crafts, Arts, Nature, Communication, Hobbies, Indoor Games, Vocational skills and Performance skills are some such examples. These interests are typically of a non-physically demanding nature and may be hobbies-, vocation- or job-related.

Skill is the learned ability to carry out a task with predetermined results often within a given amount of time, energy, or both. In other words, the abilities that one possesses. Skills can often be divided into domain-general and domain-specific skills. For example, in the domain of work, some general skills would include time management, teamwork and leadership, self-motivation and others, whereas domain-specific skills would be useful only for a certain job. Skill usually requires certain environmental stimuli and situations to assess the level of skill being shown and used.[44]

There are various forms of skills that the schools should help deliver: labour skills, life skills, people skills, social skills, soft skills, hard skills are some such examples.

Sport is not only important for children's health, it also enhances learning, achievement, resilience, psychosocial and motor development. Children who practise sports from a young age are more likely to go on doing so when they are older. School-based sports programmes can bring out noticeable positive reactions and behaviour in teens. School-based sport can be an important part of the child's overall educational experience. When students participate in sport, they can benefit not only physically, but also socially and mentally!

Sport should encourage young people to improve their personal physical performance through training and perseverance in what they like to play. Involvement in physical recreation should be an enjoyable experience, regardless of physical ability. Physical activity is vital to the holistic

---

[44]*Skill*. SlidePlayer. Retrieved July 16, 2020, from https://slideplayer.com/slide/7991460/

development of young people, fostering their physical, social and emotional health. The benefits of sport reach beyond the impact on physical well-being and the value of the educational benefits of sport should not be underestimated.

Study is applying the mind to learning and understanding a subject (especially by reading). The dictionary definition of study reads as: 'application of the mind to the acquisition of knowledge, as by reading, investigation or reflection'. This really is one aspect of growth for a young person at school.

Round Square is a worldwide association of schools on five continents sharing unique and ambitious goals. Students attending Round Square schools make a strong commitment, beyond academic excellence, to personal development and responsibility. The Round Square approach promotes six ideals of learning: Internationalism, Democracy, Environment, Adventure, Leadership and Service. These are incorporated into the curriculum throughout all member schools. Access to the Round Square network affords member schools the opportunity to arrange local and international student and teacher exchanges on a regular basis between their schools. Pupils get an opportunity to participate in local and international community service projects and conferences. Tasks tackled through the community projects include building schools, classrooms and community centres, building clean water systems for remote hill-tribes or creating and maintaining trails in National Parks. Local materials are used, and teams always work with local people ensuring that they take ownership of the work once it has been completed.

The IB offers four programmes for students aged three to 19 to help develop their intellectual, personal, emotional and social skills to live, learn and work in a rapidly globalizing world. It aims to develop inquisitive, knowledgeable and caring young people who help to create a better and more peaceful world through intercultural understanding and respect. To this end the organization works with schools, governments and international organizations to develop challenging programmes of international education and rigorous assessment. These programmes encourage students across the world to become active, compassionate and lifelong learners who understand that other people, with their differences, can also be right.

Socially Useful Productive Work (SUPW) is a subject in Indian schools where students can choose from a number of vocational education activities: embroidery and knitting, gardening, cooking, painting, carpentry and other crafts and hobbies, and clubbed community service for senior students (Class 9 onwards). Students learn to work as a team and to work with skill and deftness. It was introduced in 1978 by the Ministry of Education to promote Gandhian values and educational ideas of Mahatma Gandhi. While most private schools barring a few have dispensed with the subject, it remains an ancillary but mandatory part of course curriculum in schools affiliated to CISCE, which conducts the ICSE and the ISC examinations in India. It is also taught in some CBSE schools, which includes all Kendriya Vidyalaya and Jawahar Navodaya Vidyalaya schools.

The Fabindia School's mission is to provide access to high-quality education for boys and girls at the rural level using English as the medium of instruction. The school views primary education as a major stepping-stone towards social mobility, equality and employment opportunities. At this school there is equal emphasis on study, skill, service and sport: the school has instituted four Trophies for Excellence in Service, Skill, Sport and Study (the 4S approach). Saturday at school is the Activity Day, and on this day, regular study/academic pursuit is dispensed with in favour of service, skill and sport. To make up for the loss of the mandated study hours, the school has added one hour to the timetable from Monday to Friday.

Public schools subscribe to the philosophy that children should be exposed to a general all-round education and emerge as good secular citizens of India. Schools must develop the minds of the children and also their physique, their skills, their personality and leadership traits and create a sense of fellow feeling with their less fortunate brethren, if they are to be good citizens. Many such schools lay equal emphasis on the 4S as this alone helps young people find their true potential.

We must remember that marks (scores) do not leave marks, but 'karma' (deeds) will leave footprints on the sand. School curriculum must be built in such a way that it empowers the students and helps them make a mark in life.

Real-world Learning

Why do we have school trips? Why do we encourage visits to places of interest for our young people? Why do our parents and friends travel for leisure? Exploration and adventure are an integral part of our lives. Today the world has become smaller as we all travel to learn and experience real-world learning. A trip on a train will help us understand the difference between speed and velocity. Climbing the mountains will demonstrate the fall in air pressure as we move up the dizzying heights. Floating on the salty sea will explain what density is and how saline water offers us buoyancy!

We learn the best when we get out of the classroom and learn in the theatre with the sky above and earth below. Education is not a drill, but an experience and this is how real learning must be. We need to push young people to think out of the box, for this it is imperative that we get out of the box (classroom) too!

At my school, we were indeed very lucky to have the mid-term break and this for me personally was the best form of learning. Team building, planning, logistics, cooking, survival and most of all the need to push ourselves beyond the comfort zone made us find ourselves. The challenge always lies within. Today, when I catch up with my school friends and the hundreds of young people who have been on treks with me, they all are most thankful for the learning experiences out of school.

The challenge for us is to find the opportunity to help deliver good education, and this can only happen outside the classroom. Study is only one of the four corners of the edifice of learning, add to it service, skill and sport and you will be able to deliver quality education. Personal and social development is the key outcome of our education process. As we want the young people to grow up and become responsible and caring individuals, we must look at the real world and be able to demonstrate the outcome of learning. Away from the rote learning and into experiential learning is the preferred approach to ensure that the purpose of education is achieved.

The journey to school, stories retold and the moments you shared with your peers outside the classroom will live with you lifelong. Gripped with nostalgia, when you look back and reflect, the sports field, the school trip and the fun you had while growing up will be on the top of the mind. Yes, you will perhaps forget what you were taught in many of the subject classes, but you will remember the most caring and interesting teachers. The school trips and the adventure out of school will live with you always. You will remember an outing to a sanctuary or a bird-watching trip and this will be far more useful and real, as compared to watching the film reel or video of the same. We need to experience the real world and not rely on the reel world when we develop a curriculum for learning and education delivery.

It is not a hidden truth that many school dropouts and those who have grown up with informal learning have achieved greater heights and have found themselves. We have the case of Bill Gates among us today; earlier there were Edison and Einstein, great physicists and inventors. Many of the adventure buffs and those who have taken the course of adventure travel have been very successful in life. The world today has space for people who follow their heart and use their passion to deliver excellence in whatever they do. You do not have to live the drudgery of exams and syllabus and make a life. Self-learning and learning at one's own pace is today gaining ground too.

As experiential learning and innovative teaching takes centre stage, I am sure that real-world learning will take precedence over rote learning that mass education programmes tend to adopt. Assembly lines only produce a prototype and the earning of an average worker is a pittance as compared to the innovator, the thinker and the creator. Real life and the creation of nature must be understood, lived with and dwelt upon to offer good quality education. No school can be built with only brick and mortar; the institution of learning must be a place for our minds to wander, explore and evolve.

Today, we have the concept of a gap year, the long adventure journeys and the outings the schools and peer groups experience. This must become a part of any learning environment. As travel becomes more affordable and possible, real-world learning will become a pleasure many will be able to experience. It is not the distance covered but the need to move and explore that is needed. We do not have to go for miles, let us look in our backyards and see how we can help the young people find themselves, and this is where success will ultimately be found.

Please do appreciate the small example from real life I am

tempted to share here. In my three decades of being a youth leader and volunteer I have had the opportunity to accompany young people on adventurous journeys all over the world. We used to start our planning months in advance, the physical conditions and the benchmarks for stamina levels made us run for weeks and months to be able to qualify for the school summer camp. The days and nights spent in making our lists of food, first aid, equipment, and items of personal use were real challenges and then came the medical tests too. As I look around and try to track many of the students and those who were part of this real-world learning, I am happy to see that most of them have indeed achieved great heights and are doing very well in their lives. When we meet, they simply say that for them the opportunity to go beyond the walls of the school were indeed what made them self-sufficient and confident and helped them find themselves.

Life is an opportunity and must be lived to the fullest. Get up, get out and get going on the journey of exploration and adventure!

Today is the Day When You Define for Yourself

Decision-making is an art and fortunate are those who can do this wisely.

Education helps us decide for ourselves, by helping us experiment and find the best way ahead. There is nothing known as perfect education and what is the best decision for an individual to take. The art of decision-making is best perfected with experience and most important by the ability of an individual to take a risk and what is often referred to as 'take the call'.

Listen to the voice within before you decide for yourself, and this is the most difficult step for many of us. Many are drowned in the din and the continuous flow of thoughts that will not help you think and take the call. You can only decide if you can concentrate, and in today's world, for many young folk it will be a challenge to concentrate. To listen to yourself even in the midst of the deafening noise that's a constant in today's world is becoming increasingly difficult. We multitask, look here and see there, have peer pressure, have the want of the consumerist society pushing us, have the pressure to perform; all this makes you weak and thus you often are not able to decide for yourself.

We are at a point today where we have had to develop a

profession of Counselling, and this today seems a necessity for most of the teens and people who need to school themselves. The Counsellor is none other than your inner self. Your best counsel will never come from a person who does this for money, as they only preach and often do not even practice. Today, we have advisers, guides, mentors, gurus...and then we have followers and simply those who follow the herd! This happens as we do not listen to ourselves and make the decision. When the guru states the obvious and what we like to hear, we find this positive and feel that you can make the decision with his best advice.

Every individual is special and needs to have her/his personality developed completely and live to the fullest. To help you fulfil your very own aspirations, you have to decide for yourself, and this happens every moment. With a cool head and a warm heart, you must evaluate what is best for you and then decide. Making a decision of what to eat, what to do, where to go and many more that we feel are inconsequential moments, but what is common is that you need to decide for yourself. As we grow up, we start making our decisions, and this is what good education must empower us to do.

When we make a decision, we have pros and cons to consider, and every moment is unique for yourself, so best you breathe easy and decide for yourself and go along the road less travelled.

SECTION IV

SCHOOL LEADERSHIP

Leadership Begins and Ends at the Top

The key factors that differentiate a good school from the rest are good governance and leadership development at all levels. The Board, the staff, the students, the parent body and the community all need to be part of the leadership development ecosystem. It all begins with governance and this is where a good school leads the average.

Applying Principles of Good Governance to Schools[45]

Good governance at school builds the best environment and ensures that all the stakeholders are involved personally and emotionally in the long run. When constituting a school board, we must cover generations of members from alumni, community, institutions, business and even public service. The members must invest time and participate in the education, development and welfare of the students and teachers alike. The teachers too should be honoured on the board. Some teachers can also be invited to participate in the proceedings of the board, and be involved beyond the routine hours of work. Schools are built by philanthropy, stakeholder engagement and benefactors.

---

[45] *Governance*. Independent Schools Victoria. https://is.vic.edu.au/resource/governance/

The Board must have transparency of purpose, recognize and manage the stakeholders; this requires tact and relationship building. I am tempted to add that the schools run on relationships, relationships and relationships alone! We will examine the role of the Board/School Management Committee, the Staff, the Parents, the Community and the Students too.

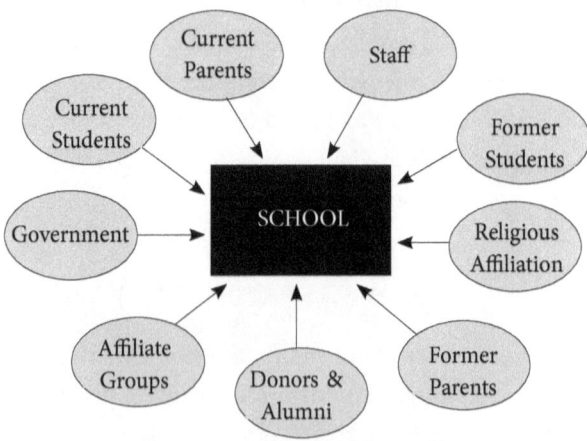

The Governing Body (Trust / Society) should be an independent body that ensures the vision of the not-for-profit schooling organization is not compromised. There must be a set of Rules and Guidelines to focus on the mission of the charity that is formed to govern the school organization. As the schools can be established by a Trust or a Society, it is imperative that there is no conflict of interest and that the school is an independent and sustainable enterprise. We have to give regard to professional acumen and the sentiment of the founders. There must be a leadership that shows a selfless concern for

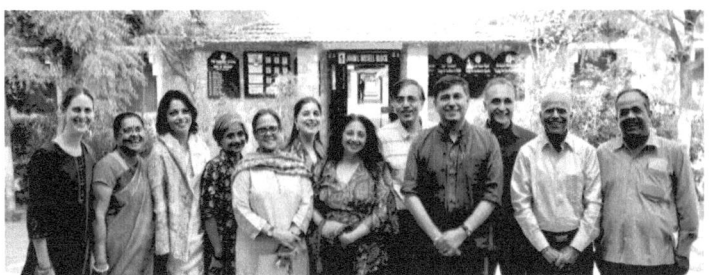

Members of the Governing Body of The Fabindia School (Photo courtesy: Neha Parmar)

the well-being of others. Setting up a school is often 'an entirely altruistic act', with an element of selfless, self-sacrificing, self-denying, compassionate, public-spirited and charitable motive. We must not forget above all it must be 'sustainable'. The Board's biggest challenge will be to become a public charity over a period of time and it is often a challenge for the investor to let go. The social enterprise will give dividend in the form of better human capital and a good citizenry and this alone is the cornerstone for a developed economy and society.

The role of the School Management Committee (SMC) in the operations of the school is very important and a good SMC will be an asset for school operations. Section 21 of the Right to Free and Compulsory Education Act 2009 (RTE), mandates the formation of School Management Committees (SMCs) in all elementary government, government-aided schools and special category schools in the country. The RTE Act envisions an SMC as the basic unit of a decentralized model of governance with active involvement of parents in the school's functioning. This body involves the parents and the community in running the school and also works as a conscience keeper for the institution. The members of the SMC should be involved in the operations of the school and assist the principal in effectively managing the school.

The School Staff should be involved beyond the classroom, and there must be a model for having them involved in the decision-making and effective functioning of the school. Clubs, societies, sports and extracurricular activities must allow the staff members to pursue their passion and lead. Right from the position of the vice principal (deputy head), the deans, heads of department, teachers and administrators, everyone must be able to envision their growth in the organization. The Staff should see a way forward in their professional careers and be empowered to make decisions at all levels. The more we delegate, the better will be our leadership at school. As teaching is a profession by chance and not by choice, we have to ensure that the staff feels much wanted and valued, this alone will bring about a change from average to the leaders that they must become. The most important step is building learning communities and the teachers must join organizations like Learning Forward or ASCD (Association for Supervision and Curriculum Development) find out how to plan, implement, and measure high-quality professional learning so that the team can achieve success with the school system.

Good schools have a good Parent Teacher Association (PTA), and the school is actually a partnership of parents and teachers to build an ecosystem for children to develop emotionally and intellectually. The children must care for the environment, care for the community and care for the country;

this is only possible when the family and the institutions work for the betterment of the young people. Today most teachers rue the fact that parents have little or no time for their children as they have to juggle their lives between profession and economic necessity of a family. This makes the role of a PTA even more paramount as parents can together work to help each other in addition to depending on just the teacher/tutor to lead the learning process. In good schools, the parents are involved effectively and this is the key factor in contributing to the making of a good school. The students at school and the alumni must also be involved in institution building.

Public Schools lay emphasis on an all-round education. To develop latent talents and skills, a variety of hobbies are offered and the choice of one per year out of photography, art, pottery, sculpture, carpentry, metalwork, electronics, aero-modelling, philately, etc. is made compulsory. In addition, to build talent and develop leadership abilities these schools are well organized in debating, dramatics, music and have special interest societies in disciplines such as astronomy, wildlife, literary affairs, history and human rights, etc. Schools endeavour to have their own student-run publications, newsletters and magazines.

The prefect system and a strong adventure programme (mountain climbing, river swimming and other outward-bound activities) inculcate character and leadership. Good citizenship is inculcated by the actual practice of democracy in letting the students run all these activities. A care and concern for their fellow human beings and for the environment is created by a strong social service programme which includes working in the villages, going on disaster relief expeditions, working with the blind, deaf, dumb and mentally challenged, working on tree planting, gardening, compost pit making, etc.

The alumni association is an association of graduates or, more broadly, of former students of the institution. These associations often organize social events, publish newsletters or magazines and raise funds for the organization. Many provide a variety of benefits and services that help alumni maintain connections to their educational institution and fellow graduates. Additionally, such groups often support fresh alumni, and provide a forum to form new friendships and business relationships with people of similar background. This network is the most important determinant of the brand value of a good school.

The Making of a Good School:

- Student centric—prime focus on the needs of the students, their interests, strengths and what goes into making every child succeed.
- Strong fundamentals—offer the best of learning to enhance numeracy, literacy, critical thinking, character building and work to develop a child in a holistic manner.
- Positive school experience—a child must be a lifelong learner and develop confidence through a positive school experience.
- Good teachers—caring and competent teachers build a great school experience, their compassion and the ability to help every child is most crucial.
- Parents and community—need to involve all the stakeholders. As the school is a social place, it is imperative to have good relations with the community.

- Diversity, inclusion and belonging—a good school offers opportunity to all students regardless of family and background.

Leadership at the school is a major catalyst in helping build a good school. Promoters and social entrepreneurs have to think beyond just investment and the ROI (return on investment). The school works for the future generations and crystal ball gazing is not easy at all. A student may end up for 15 years in a particular school, and to prepare a child for a decade or two ahead is the most complex task and not a mere economic enterprise. Developing strong vision and mission statements can help stakeholders in your school reach such a common understanding. This can only be achieved by ensuring that we build leadership at school at all levels.

Principal as the Chief Learning Leader

Should the principal be the chief executive officer (CEO) with due qualification and degrees? Are owner-driven schools, which look at the school purely as a business enterprise, better than schools run by charities? Such questions always make us think and we do debate this matter often. Many good schools are owner-driven and the owners may not have the qualifications required to be the principal. What is most important, however, is that the principal/head of the school should be the chief learning leader (CLL).

Learning is the act of acquiring new, or modifying and reinforcing existing knowledge, behaviours, skills, values, or preferences and may involve synthesizing different types of information. The ability to learn is possessed by humans, animals and some machines. Progress over time tends to follow learning curves. Learning is not compulsory; it is contextual. It does not happen all at once, but builds upon and is shaped by what we already know. To that end, learning may be viewed as a process, rather than a collection of factual and procedural knowledge.[46]

The learning institution is always in evolution and is able to understand the needs of the pupils and deliver to the

---

[46]Bhondekar, R.D. *Love—The Key to Optimism: Path towards Happiness*. (2015). Notion Press.

happiness of all stakeholders. What is imperative is that the CLL must understand that knowledge is not just information and acquiring of skills, but a road to infinite possibility and its growth alone is the single most need for an evolving mind. For the head to be held high, and true freedom be experienced, the learning institution must ensure that the CLL must be a person who leads by example. Simply having a degree or certification is not enough, learning is a never-ending process and it is the only way to build schools that learn.

In *Schools that Learn*, Peter Senge argues that teachers, administrators, and other members of school communities must learn how to build their own capacity; that is, they must develop the capacity to learn. From Senge's perspective, real improvement will only occur if the people responsible for implementation design the change itself: 'It is becoming clear that schools can be re-created, made vital, and sustainably renewed not by fiat or command, and not by regulation, but by taking the learning orientation.' The principal/CLL must be able to motivate, coach, inspire, teach, mentor, be a visionary, ensure teamwork and above all lead by example.

Education is simply building your own capacity. This must be the goal of each individual, including the CLL. Senge makes a powerful argument regarding the need for a systems approach and learning orientation by introducing *Schools that Learn* with a historical perspective on educational systems. Specifically, he details 'industrial age' assumptions about both learning—that 'children are deficient and schools should fix them', that learning is strictly an intellectual enterprise, that everyone should learn in the same way, that classroom learning is distinctly different than that occurring outside of school, and that some kids are smart while others are not—and schools 'are run by specialists who maintain control', knowledge is inherently fragmented, schools teach some kind of objective truth, and 'learning is primarily individualistic and competition accelerates learning'. These assumptions about learning and the nature and purpose of schools reflect deeply embedded cultural beliefs that must be considered, and in many cases directly confronted, if schools are to develop the learning orientation necessary for improvement.

The CLL must set the tone for the growth and development of a dynamic school. The world today offers a great opportunity to learn and grow; information flow is no more hierarchical and knowledge today is in free flow mode. In a world without barriers working to reach new frontiers in technology and learning, there is really no way that the school can do without a CLL. Be it the principal or the owner, they will only succeed if they work like a CLL. The business world CEO may have the KRA (Key Result Areas) model and look at every outcome as a measure, and this will have its limitation in the working of a good school. The CLL will have priorities and will understand that the learning institution generates wealth that is far more than the simple surplus in income and expenses, and it is not the top-line alone that matters. Education thus is not a commodity but an infinitesimal wealth. The understanding of infinitesimals was a major roadblock, and today the mathematical world has evolved and we have even begun to look at the creative infinite mind. The wisdom and the ability to be a learner is all that a CLL needs to be.

Good governance and active participation of all

stakeholders in a school—the management, the teachers, the community, the students and the head—is very much needed to build a learning organization. The role of the CLL is indeed a complex one and no job description is perfect for the head of the school. The leader must not be one decorated with a degree alone. It is imperative the leader must lead as the role so demands. Lead by example for the teachers, the students and the community.

The CLL has to create an environment for learning and a culture of self-discipline. In the corporate world a Chief Learning Officer (CLO) is the highest-ranking corporate officer in charge of learning management. CLOs can be experts in corporate or personal training, with degrees in education, instructional design, business or similar fields. The CLL, as we describe the head of the school, is at an even higher pedestal than the CLO. The CLL, beyond being a person well-versed in the field, must have knowledge of administration and be a good manager too.

In 'Role of the Principal', Derrick Meador states:

> The role of the principal covers many different areas including leadership, teacher evaluation, student discipline and many others. Being an effective principal is hard work and is also time-consuming. A good principal is balanced within all their roles and works hard to ensure that they are doing what they feel is best for all constituents involved. ... A school principal is the primary leader in a school building. A good leader always leads by example. A principal should be positive, enthusiastic, have their hand in the day to day activities of the school, and listen to what their constituents are

> saying. An effective leader is available to teachers, staff members, parents, students, and community members. Good leaders stay calm in difficult situations, think before they act, and put the needs of the school before themselves. An effective leader steps up to fill in holes as needed, even if it isn't a part of their daily routine.[47]

Effective leadership is taking along with you all the stakeholders of the school. The key challenge for the CLL is to be able to lead as per the vision of the school, ensure there is good governance and quality delivery of education at the school. A large part of any school principal's job is to handle student discipline. Most principals are also responsible for evaluating their teachers' performances following district and state guidelines. Developing, implementing and evaluating the programmes within the school is another large part of a school principal's role. A principal should review, remove, rewrite or write policies and procedures every year as needed. Having an effective student handbook can improve the quality of education the students receive. It can also make a principal's job a little easier. The principal's role is to make sure students, teachers and parents know what these policies and procedures are and to hold each individual accountable to following them.

Having good relations with parents and community members can benefit the principal in a variety of areas. If you have built trusting relationships with a parent whose child has a discipline issue, then it makes it easier to deal with the

---

[47]Meador, D. *The role of the principal in schools.* Academia.edu-Share research. Retrieved 23 June 2020, from https://www.academia.edu/35820393/The_Role_of_the_Principal_in_Schools_by_Derrick_Meador_Updated

situation if the parent supports the school and your decision. The same holds true for the community. Building relationships with individuals and businesses in the community can help your school tremendously. Benefits include donations, personal time and overall positive support for your school. It is a vital part of any principal's job to nurture their relationships with parents and community members.

Learning is a ladder with countless number of steps that we must keep climbing, and this is most essential for the CLL. Set higher standards for yourself, then alone you will be able to lead schools that learn.

Student Leader: Mentor or Monitor?

It is a major challenge for the class teacher to find the best monitor for the class, one who can help discipline the class, lead the class and be the role model. We really need to have in place the leader who can inspire, must value his position and commit to be disciplined. Monitors are often high-handed, are unable to live up to the position of responsibility and be impartial in their delivery. The authority of the teacher may not be a sufficient deterrent power at hand with the class monitor. We need an opinion-maker, a leader, an individual best suited for being a mentor, in place of a monitor.

When the cat's away, the mice are out to play! This often happens when a class teacher steps out of the classroom and young people are left to themselves for a while. In such situations, it is the monitor who admonishes, cautions or reminds his/her classmates, especially with respect to matters of conduct. A monitor is also defined as 'a pupil who assists a teacher in routine duties'. A wise and trusted counsellor or teacher is a mentor. It is a mentor who is best suited to lead us and not the monitor who is there to only watch the students and goad them. Class monitors have the rights and duties to assist the class and subject teachers to maintain a good order in their own classroom.

Monitors as supervisors are required to lead by example

(modelling, mentoring and influencing) such that their classmates stay ethically robust in their work, fostering practice wisdom and ethical maturity. At times, supervisors may also be working with people who struggle in this regard; indeed supervisors may also struggle themselves.

Mentoring today has even become a profession. Most of us look up to a guru, a leader who will leave footsteps on the sand for us as 'marg darshan'. Mentoring is a powerful personal development and empowerment tool. It is an effective way of helping people to progress in their careers and is becoming increasing popular as its potential is realized.

A mentor may be a peer. When we think of our days at school, we will find some individual who really held our hand and did more than just a monitor could in a class. In school often students help each other to sail through many tough times. From class work and assignments to emotional support, the role of a peer as a mentor is very important. A monitor must be a mentor, his circle of influence must be beyond a small group, for then alone the class will look up to the student leader.

A Monitor in Classroom, a Mentor for Life?

Who should you choose to lead your class? Having the best set of prefects in a school or putting in place a School Council is always a major task in every calendar year for the school staff. How to find a monitor who can be a mentor? We have a list of attributes. This isn't an exhaustive list, but it will help you make your own list of attributes. Based on your list, you need to find the best individual to be the leader of the class, group or a house in the school.

- **Peer pressure**: A young person will first succumb to pressure from friends and individuals he or she has in the circle of friends and well-wishers. This is a big challenge, a test and even the single most issue in terms of delivering discipline or leadership in a class.
- **Value system:** It is the key to assess an individual's integrity and ability to be valued.
- **Physical strength:** It may look as a way to have delivery with brute force. This is often not a good way to find the best person to supervise or monitor a group.
- **Excellence in study:** Overachievers in academics are often too committed to their cause and will not really want to be the leader you need.
- **Individual with a skill:** Potential leaders, they may, however, sometimes be perceived as a bit eccentric!
- **Good in a sport**: This could be the quality of a team builder. The individual's lack of performance in the class may not make them the best mentor. Often those who participate in sports have a great following and are able to drum up a band of cheerleaders.
- **Great at communication:** Such an individual will be a motivator, but not always the true deliverer.
- **One who tries to appease the teacher**: This individual may often be referred to as one who appeases for selfish needs and is not appreciated much by peers.
- **Child of a person of influence:** Such an individual often gets to be a monitor, but may not be the best choice as a mentor.

- **Compassionate and loving:** Individuals who make the best mentors and great monitors too, for they are able to win friends and influence people.

The challenges above and the need to develop students as good leaders is what we really need to look at. Mentor or monitor, it is the real leader who can deliver and make the true difference in leading by compulsion or leading by example.

The student leader must be a mentor, not simply the one who will be the monitor or 'minds a class'. We need to look at the attributes of good student leadership to be able to find the best mentor for the class, instead of appointing a class monitor to merely supervise and be the Pied Piper.

Essential Qualities for a Student Leader

- Integrity: Leaders must be true to themselves. Leaders who behave consistently with their value system inspire trust in their followers and are seen as honest. Leaders need to know themselves well to be true to their values as well as to create a vision for their group that comes from the heart.
- Autonomy: Leaders must be self-directed. Individuals who can act without an authoritative figure telling them what to do each step of the way can make the decisions necessary to move their group along towards its goals. Leaders need to see options, make choices and solve problems in order to direct themselves and others.
- Group dynamics: Leaders must involve group members. Those who assign tasks appropriately to followers and incorporate group members' ideas into the group vision recognise that they cannot be leaders without followers.

- Human relations: Leaders must use the human touch. Individuals who create an organizational environment in which all participants feel welcome, respected and valued, are exercising their power well, can maintain group membership and energy work well.
- Positioning: Leaders must see the big picture. Leaders need to know which tasks require the help of those outside their own group.
- Task effectiveness: Leaders must get the job done. Competent leaders match tasks to followers' abilities and motivations, provide training and understand time management.

These may seem very hard to find in the average student and as much a challenge for the average teacher to spot too. Task delivery is undoubtedly the key point in finding the right person for the right assignment.

Prefects and class monitors as mentors are members of the student body who have to be chosen as good role models for others and are willing to help make the school a safer place too. They play a very important role in taking ahead the mission of the school.

Smart Teachers Make Smart Classes

Smart classrooms are technology-enhanced classrooms that foster opportunities for teaching and learning by integrating learning technology, such as computers, specialised software, audience response technology, assistive listening devices, networking, and audio/visual capabilities.

Smart Classrooms or Smart Teachers?

One may ask whether 'Smart Classrooms' can, by themselves, improve learning, or whether there are other ways to improve learning.

As it is the people who make a place, so a classroom is what the teacher and students want it to be. No amount of technology and IT solutions will ever be able to replace smart teachers. The best of classrooms need the best of teachers to make learning fun and also ensure quality delivery. All the hardware and software will soon be outdated and you will be the scapegoat for the marketer who will continue to sell you the illusion of smarter classrooms!

Teachers make the world of a child better, as beyond just learning, many students imbibe the values and mannerisms of their gurus. Technology may be the tool, however, the teacher alone is the effective delivery agent for quality learning in the classroom.

We often hear people say that money alone cannot make the difference. Any amount or money spent on teaching aides and infrastructure will never be able to replace a good teacher in the classroom. The challenge lies in finding the best teachers and taking good care of their need for resources, comfort and well-being.

In the ancient times the guru or the smart teacher was supreme and the shishya or student would do all they could to win the favour of the guru, go to any lengths to give the 'Gurudakshina, an offering that was part of the tradition of repaying one's teacher or guru after a period of study, the completion of formal education or one's spiritual guidance. This tradition was borne out of the need to acknowledge, respect and thank one's guru. A form of reciprocity and exchange between student and teacher, the repayment was not exclusively monetary and could also be a special task the teacher wanted the student to accomplish. This system was based on the philosophy that the guru is the real catalyst for learning and he alone could make a real difference. Here it was not the smart class but the smart teacher who brought about the transformation. The teacher's role in the life of the student was considered paramount, and thus the gurudakshina philosophy laid emphasis on the fact the teacher must be very well looked after.

Innovative teachers do not rely on technology and are not excessively dependent on the smart classroom. A smart teacher is one who is innovative and makes learning fun in the simplest of locations.

Many years ago, I had the opportunity of being part of a Train-the-Trainer workshop. Our group was put up in a very basic lodging away from the nearest village or town, in the Australian outback and this is where I had the privilege of experiencing how it was the smart teacher alone and not the smart classroom that could make effective learning a reality. We had no classroom or training area, no power, no tools, no PowerPoint presentations and even no chalk and blackboard! We, however, had one of the smartest trainers to lead us for the five-day training period. I transformed into a trainer and was able to conduct and help deliver over one hundred training workshops, and empower thousands of youth leaders and teachers all over the world. Thank you to my guru whom I have not named; I am sure my thanks will reach her always.

When we look at the needs of the modern world, it is good teachers who make the difference. Most schools in India are funded and run by the government. However, the public education system faces serious challenges including a lack of adequate infrastructure, insufficient funding, a shortage of staff and scarce facilities. In 2012, the Annual Status of Education Report (ASER) found that, in rural India, the number of children in the age group of 6-14 years attending private schools was 28 per cent only. James Tooley in his study states: 'The schools studied were found to be providing good quality education in the English medium, at costs which were affordable to the poorest of families. These schools were run with minimum resources and teachers were hired on contract.'[48] Despite the fact that the teachers were paid much lower salaries compared to government school teachers, these

---

[48]Tooley, J. *The Beautiful Tree: A Personal Journey into How the World's Poorest People Are Educating Themselves.* (2009). Penguin India.

schools delivered better as the people had to perform.

The need of the hour is smart teachers. With the poor skill-building environment, the bigger challenge is not of finding smart classrooms but of finding smart teachers. After all, the smart classes will also need smart teachers to deliver! The low wages paid to the teachers as well as teaching not really being the preferred profession make smart teachers almost hard to find. As a school improvement coach, I work for helping schools deliver affordable quality education, and the key for our success lies in the schools valuing the human resource at a premium and keeping over 60 per cent of their operation cost for salaries alone. As we move to low fee schools, this cost may even go way beyond 60 per cent. A good school needs the smart teacher and their technology is that of mind and heart and not of brick-and-mortar tools.

Good teachers are hard to get, as teaching apart from not being a very sought-after profession is also an underpaid one. Add to this the woes of poor training and learning environment and the woeful lack of innovative programmes for training teachers. You will find out that the way to make a good school is by having smart teachers and not merely having smart classes. The school experience is the key for the personal and social development of a young person. We need an environment with a heart and a soul and not simply a brick-and-mortar campus.

Smart people make smart choices, and smart schools have to go beyond smart classrooms! The reality is that effective teaching goes much beyond developing subject matter expertise. From my experiences in the education sector, great teachers share two common characteristics: an extraordinary sense of humility and a strong commitment to continual improvement, based upon the fundamental motivation to inspire students to succeed.

Conclusion: My Good School—When Passion Meets Education

My Good School offers the model for a tailor-made school experience, altering the environment by empowering students and focussing on personal and social development with the help of different stakeholders, namely, teachers, management and the community at large.

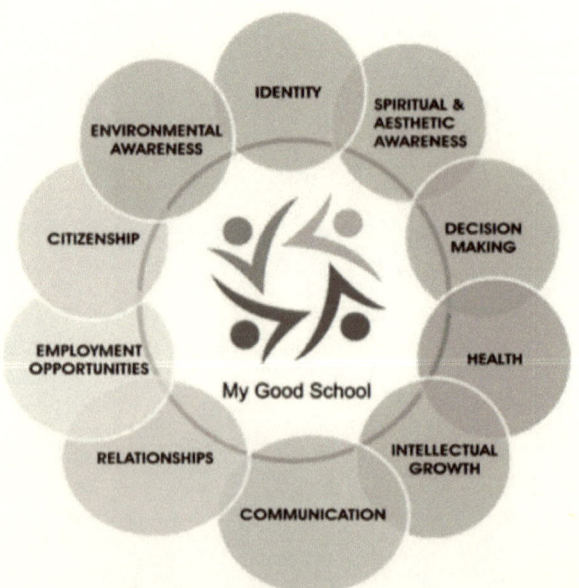

This philosophy of quality in education is about offering an environment where experiential learning is made possible through activities beyond just study, brings to life learning that would otherwise be theoretical and uncoordinated. We have demonstrated that learning can be easily personalised, and assessment must be a fun process to leave a lifelong impact.

The Education System

Both government and private schools face several challenges:

- Students and teachers might be insensitive to their surroundings due to lack of awareness.
- 'Spoon-feeding' culture: students are almost entirely dependent on their teachers and are not being creative.
- Students and teachers have a lack of interaction beyond school.
- Students have limited knowledge beyond the scope of their curriculum.
- Rigid school schedules force students to focus on academics and stops them from exploring their interests.
- Many schools are unaware that their environment might be unhealthy for some students and teachers because often, we do not see failure as an opportunity to grow and learn.

The Solution—My Good School standard core curriculum:

Personal Identity	Spiritual & Aesthetic Awareness
Self-awareness, -esteem, -image, -confidence	Including moral development; values; appreciating Arts; memorable experiences.
Decision-Making	**Health**
Based on access to information, advice counselling, with appropriate support. Taking responsibility for learning and development.	Including sex education, fitness, sports.
Intellectual Growth	**Social Communication Skills**
Professional Learning Program (PLP) curriculum, information technology.	Involving problem solving, planning.
Relationships	**Employability Skills**
Linked to responsibilities, empathy and teamwork.	Vocational development, employability
Citizenship	**Environmental Awareness**
Community and political awareness and involvement; rights and responsibilities	Awareness and responsibilities

The 'My Good School' curriculum works for the 'Personal and Social Development of every Individual' by creating a suitable learning environment for students and teachers alike. It encourages schools to focus on Service, Skill, Sport and Study, so that they can grow as individuals.

Service-Skill-Sport-Study

Global implications of My Good School (MGS)

With the world today focusing on 'Social and Emotional Learning' (SEL), the MGS helps:

- Builds a greater engagement between stakeholders and this builds empathy and trust
- Provides space for mentorship to the teachers and community members
- Helps provide young people with skills to prepare them for the world, this includes vocational and social skills

College Readiness

Similar to what the Duke of Edinburgh's Award, Outward Bound, Scouts & Guides and similar programmes do for mainstream and residential school with a focus on Middle and Secondary Schools, My Good School works with a whole child approach for learning and reflection. It uses the experience of extra-curricular and sport activity and provides a structure to monitor the outcome.

Appreciation of One Another

My Good School not only encourages students to focus on experiential learning but also focuses on helping its teachers, institution management the community at large. The four sections (Service, Skill, Sport and Study) offer the opportunity to provide a learning experience to all; this makes way for involving the students and the community to not only discover new talent but also help a young person work to explore possibilities for careers post-school.

As Rajeshree Shihag, principal of The Fabindia School, puts it: 'With the My Good School curriculum the passionate teachers, management, community and the students with common areas of interest in hobbies and activities collaborate beyond the classroom, thus working to help each other excel and work to better learning outcomes.'

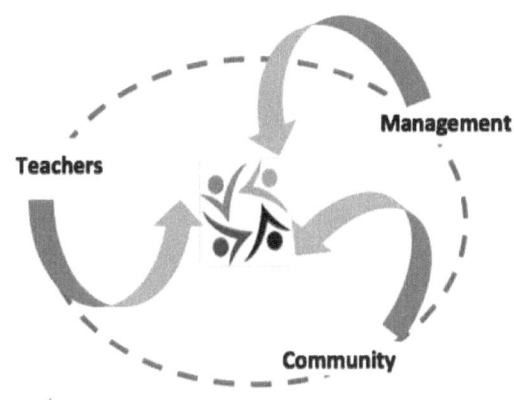

Impact

- Empowers students by creating an environment for their personal and social development.
- Encourages students to become involved in activities beyond just study; this helps develop confidence, knowledge and networks.
- Experiential learning is a critical factor in the student's progressing successfully through adolescence.

Index

academic, 15, 36, 39, 58, 76, 85, 126, 128
activities, 9, 15, 30, 45, 53, 77, 108, 116, 123, 127, 141, 161, 165
administration, 10, 15, 41, 58, 124, 140, 145, 147
adolescence, 10, 64, 165
affiliated, 31–33, 38, 127
affordable, 6, 8–10, 42, 157, 158
all-round, 6, 33, 128, 141
alumni, 77, 137, 138, 141, 142
annual day, 75, 77–79
Annual Status of Education Report (ASER), 157
assessment, 20, 22, 23, 35, 95, 96, 127, 161

behaviour, 9, 53, 63, 95, 114, 125
boarding school, 6, 109
book, 33, 35, 62–65

career, 29, 41, 52, 85, 120, 140, 151
Centre for Science and Environment (CSE), viii
Cambridge International Examinations, 31, 32
Certificate in Vocational Education (CVE), 31
Central Board of Secondary Education (CBSE), 6, 20, 31–35, 37–39, 123, 127
Chief Learning Leader (CLL), 144–49
Chief Learning Officer (CLO), 147
cognitive, 80, 94, 107
colleges, 18, 31, 37, 38, 92
communication, 10, 64, 70, 80, 152, 162
competition, 18, 21, 67, 69, 146
confidence, 9, 43, 53, 64, 103, 105, 107, 142, 162, 165
Council for the Indian School Certificate Examinations (CISCE), 6, 31, 34, 35, 37–39, 123, 127
culture, 42, 69, 81, 84, 105, 161
curriculum, 9, 10, 14, 15, 30, 33, 36, 40, 56, 66, 86, 99, 128, 161, 162

design, 15, 66–69, 145

emotional, 5, 48, 94, 103, 107, 126, 151, 163
employability, 10, 162
employment, 8, 112, 127
English-medium, 8, 95
evaluation, 13, 33–35, 83, 147
examination, 18, 31, 34, 35
examinations, 6, 31, 32, 35, 127
experiential, 8, 9, 15, 39, 87, 88, 130, 131, 161, 164, 165
extracurricular, 34, 140

faculty, 95
failure, 17, 116, 161
family, 5, 23, 48, 63, 103, 141

Gandhi, Mahatma, 69, 127
government, 6, 31, 138, 139, 157, 158, 161
guru, 30, 55, 56, 69, 151, 156

homework, 6, 32, 48, 49, 96, 109

Indian Certificate of Secondary Education (ICSE), 31–35, 37–39, 127
International Award for Young People (IAYP), i, vii
International Baccalaureate (IB), 7, 31, 32, 34, 126
International General Certificate Examination (IGCSE), 34
Indian School Certificate (ISC), 31

Jawahar Navodaya Vidyalaya, 127
job, 55–57, 125, 148, 149, 154

Kendriya Vidyalaya, 127
kindergarten, 44, 45, 51, 119
Kozyra, Pat, 48, 49, 62, 75, 117

language, 30, 35, 38, 70, 112
leadership, xviii, 25, 26, 29, 39, 65, 76, 83, 84, 96, 99, 105, 125, 126, 141, 143, 148, 153
Learning Forward, 26, 140
liberal arts, 86–90, 92
library, 63, 65

Macaulay, 30
madrasa, 31
management, 10, 41, 42, 56, 138, 147, 160, 164
methodology, 5, 14, 17, 23, 38
Montessori, 7, 44

National Council of Educational Research and Training (NCERT), 31, 35
National Council for Teacher Education (NCTE), 32
National Foundation of Education Research, 20

National Institute of Open
  Schooling (NIOS), 31
National University of
  Educational Planning and
  Administration (NUEPA), 32
New Education Policy 2020,
  31, 32
newsletter, 74, 141, 142
newspaper, 19, 62, 63

organisation, 27, 56, 97, 127,
  138, 140, 142, 147
owner-driven, 144

performance, 18, 19, 21–24, 35,
  84, 98, 100
personality, 86, 107, 128, 134

qualitative evaluation, 34
qualitative measure, 98
quantitative measure, 98

read, 7, 49, 61–65
research, 15, 34, 65, 72, 88, 95
residential school, 16, 109, 163
Right to Free and Compulsory
  Education Act 2009 (RTE),
  139

scholarships, 42
School Management Committee
  (SMC), 139, 140
Secondary School Certificate
  (SSC), 32–34
syllabus, 33, 35, 57, 131
Service, Skill, Sport and Study,
  vii, x, 10, 14, 76, 100, 123,
  128, 162, 164

Tagore, Rabindranath, 7, 54,
  69, 86
The Doon School, vii, xi, 28, 39,
  74, 123, 124
The Duke of Edinburgh's Award,
  vii, 7, 163
time management, 41, 73,
  108–11, 125, 154
timetable, 16, 109, 128
training, 15, 27, 29, 41, 42, 84,
  95, 154, 157, 158

UNESCO, 8

Vivekananda, Swami, 7, 121

www.ingramcontent.com/pod-product-compliance
Lightning Source LLC
Chambersburg PA
CBHW031927240526
45464CB00023B/1728